ROSS COUNTY

From Highland League to Hampden

ROSS COUNTY

From Highland League to Hampden

———

FRANK GILFEATHER

BIRLINN

First published in 2010 by
Birlinn Limited
West Newington House
10 Newington Road
Edinburgh
EH9 1QS

www.birlinn.co.uk

ISBN: 978 1 84158 921 3

British Library Cataloguing-in-Publication Data
A catalogue record for this book is available
from the British Library

Designed and typeset by Mark Blackadder

Printed and bound by Bell & Bain Ltd, Glasgow

CONTENTS

THEY DARED TO DREAM

Ross County made their way to Scottish football's national stadium in search of a miracle. They sought to become the first club outside the game's top flight to lift the Scottish Cup since 1938. They were hungry for the ultimate prize and desperate to achieve the impossible dream of securing a place in European football on behalf of the people of the Highlands.

It may have been the theme song of their opponents for the occasion, but 'Love is in the Air' encapsulated the mood in and around Hampden as 20,000 County supporters from all over the world gathered on a sunny spring afternoon to back their heroes against Dundee United in the Scottish Cup final of 15 May 2010.

It was a defining moment in the history of the First Division club from Dingwall, whose path to the ultimate round of the competition saw them grapple with, and defeat, two of the Scottish Premier League's Goliaths, Hibernian and Celtic.

They had already dared to dream a few weeks earlier when they ventured south to face Celtic, a club steeped in history and tradition, and with a trophy cabinet packed with honours and a squad of highly-paid players from the upper echelons of football.

The Hoops' hopes of salvaging a season which had seen them trail their arch rivals Rangers in the quest for the Premier League championship were shattered by County, whose performance in winning the semi-final offered everyone connected with the club belief that the Scottish Cup could eventually sit in the Victoria Park boardroom.

Whatever was to happen in the final, however, there was the realisation throughout the club that nothing would ever be quite the same.

The Ross County Football Club story started when a group of officials from the local amateur side, Dingwall Victors, became keen to push for entry to the Highland League, and secured their place at the beginning of the 1929–30 season.

There was a new government at Westminster, with the Labour Party winning most seats in the Commons for the first time, though they did not have a majority. Ramsay MacDonald, born in Lossiemouth, Moray, the illegitimate child of a farm labourer and a housemaid, took his place in history as Labour's first prime minister in an election in which women under the age of 30 were permitted to vote for the first time.

Earlier that year, stories crossed the Atlantic of the Valentine's Day

ROSS COUNTY

*From Highland League
to Hampden*

Massacre when seven gangsters, rivals of the notorious mobster Al Capone, were gunned down in Chicago. It was the year that Alexander Fleming discovered penicillin and Buster Keaton and Laurel & Hardy were making people laugh with their antics on the silver screen.

In the two years leading up to the start of the 1929–30 season, there were all manner of fund-raising activities in Dingwall and across Ross-shire: dances, concerts and other events, all designed to aid the club's finances in those first uncertain steps in their new world.

A matter of three months after the beginning of the football season, the economic disaster that was to become known as the Great Depression swept across the United States and beyond following the collapse of the New York Stock Exchange. Wall Street was about to crash.

By then, Ross County was already a fresh presence in football, though the club was still in its embryonic phase. A section of Jubilee Park in the town was bought and became the new club's home, later to be re-named Victoria Park in deference to their predecessors, and when they kicked-off their existence on 15 August 1929, the newly-formed team did so against an Inverness League select, a game watched by 1,200 fans and which ended 2–2.

The home side's team, captained by Tom Pirie, a former Queen's Park and Aberdeen player, that momentous day was: Gray, Munro, Johnston; McLeman, Pirie, Grant; Scott, Trail, Morrison, Mackenzie, Young.

A club crest featured the Caberfeidh, or Stag's Head, from the regimental badge of the Seaforth Highlanders, the regiment aligned to the area and in which many locals had fought and died during the First and Second World Wars. The Stag's Head brought with it the team's nickname, the Staggies.

It is worth recording that the Seaforth Highlanders were created with the amalgamation of the 72nd Highlanders (Duke of Albany's Own) and the 78th Highlanders (Ross-shire Buffs) in reform of the British Army in 1881. Later mergers followed until 2006, when all Scottish Infantry Regiments came together to form the Royal Regiment of Scotland.

The regiment, and its predecessors, boasted a number of Victoria Cross winners, among them Major John Mackenzie, from Contin, Ross-shire. A 29-year-old sergeant in the 2nd Battalion, he was honoured for his bravery in leading a charge against the enemy while wounded at Dompoassi, Ashanti – now Ghana – on 6 June 1900.

The courage of Lance-Corporal Robert McBeath, from Kinlochbervie, Sutherland, was recognised after he volunteered to deal with a nest of machine-gunners during the Battle of Cambrai in France on 20 November 1917. He captured three officers and 30 men, while Major-General Sir Herbert MacPherson, from Ardersier, was 30 years old and a lieutenant in the 78th Highlanders during the Indian Mutiny of 1857, when he was honoured for his bravery at the siege of Lucknow.

There were others in that famous regiment, iconic and brave figures who made the Highlands proud. Could this new football club, in some small way, inspire the people of Ross-shire and the Highlands in general?

In that first, tentative season, County won the North of Scotland Cup,

The Ross County team that won the North of Scotland Cup in their first season in the Highland League. (*Dingwall Museum*)

beating Clachnacuddin and Inverness Caledonian en route to the final against Elgin City on the neutral but snow-covered ground of Telford Street Park, in the Highland capital, Inverness. County won the day, and the cup, by two goals to one.

Over the decades that followed, they produced a long list of teams that graced the Highland League, winning three championships, in 1967, 1991, and again the following season.

That initial Highland League triumph came in the era of the BBC Light programme, the release of The Beatles' *Sgt Pepper's Lonely Hearts Club Band*, the completion by Sir Francis Chichester of his round-the-world, one-man sail-boat achievement, and the attack by 50,000 Vietcong and North Vietnamese forces on Saigon.

The County team in those days was made up largely of players who lived locally, and Sandy Wallace, once a right back with the club and later its manager, recalled that success: 'What I remember about that season was that we really were a team; we all knew each other's talents and limitations and played accordingly. 'There was a smattering of real ability there as well, with ex-seniors like Jimmy Hosie, Don MacMillan and later, Jackie Lornie, and of course we got the little bit of luck that every team needs to be successful.'

The two other Highland League titles were won under the leadership of Bobby Wilson, formerly a cultured right back with Dundee and a coach who

The County squad
in 1966–67

(Back left–right):
Frank Thomson (chairman),
David Hamilton,
Dennis Laughton,
Sandy Wallace,
Peter Borley,
Ian Greig,
Hamish Fraser,
Jack Lornie,
Don MacMillan,
Gordon Davidson,
Colin Brett,
Chic Ogilvie.

(Front left–right):
Tommy 'Tucker' Thomson,
Sandy MacKenzie,
Ian McNeill,
Jim Hosie,
Calum Grant,
Ian Davidson.

had managed successfully in the Highland League with Keith, with whom he won three championships.

An unsuccessful spell in charge at Raith Rovers saw Wilson relieved of his position and he was working as chief scout at Dunfermline Athletic when Ross County's then chairman, the ebullient Morris Newton, invited him to take over the reins at Victoria Park.

'I signed up in July 1987 at a time when County were holding up the rest of the Highland League as the bottom club,' said Bobby. 'I felt it was a great challenge because when I was at Keith, Ross County were always one of the better sides in the Highland League. Johnny Buchanan, who had played with them before moving to Cardiff City and then re-joining County, was the manager from whom I took over, and Jock McDonald, the legendary Highland League and SFA administrator, recommended me for the job.

'Knowing I was to take over, I had gone to have a look at them against Inverness Caledonian at Telford Street during the season before, and I decided I would keep just five of our 14-man squad. It was a massive clear-out. I brought in Chris Somerville, from Golspie, a right back I'd remembered from when he was at Dunfermline, and Billy Ferries, a right winger who, in my view, could have played at a much higher level. I also had my eye on Gordon Connelly, whom I'd had as a youth at Dunfermline. He was a central midfielder and I wanted to build my team round him.

'Things improved as I brought in better players. I wanted to build a good unit rather than have any so-called star players or prima donnas.'

Wilson and the club tried to sign the players they wanted on one-year contracts with a year's option and a wage of just £1 a week, but they were told by the SFA that a ruling of the day did not permit that. The club would have

to cough-up more than £156 a year to a player if he was required to sign such an agreement.

'I was thinking about those players I knew I would have to pay higher signing-on fees, and so I had to keep a close eye my budget,' Wilson recalled. 'In the end, we paid them the princely sum of £4 a week.

'It was an exciting time. I was the only full-time employee and I pulled in Davie Jackson as my assistant, and Don Cowie, the father of Don, who went from Ross County to Inverness Caledonian Thistle and then to Watford in the Championship in England, was the real experienced presence I needed in the centre of defence.

'It all got slowly better. I had started a soccer academy at the park every Sunday morning with about 150 youngsters joining in. And we hit upon a rather clever marketing ploy by giving each kid a free ticket for home games. The train of thought was that their dads would have to take them to Victoria Park. It was then up to me to keep them by producing a good, entertaining and winning team.'

With two league titles in the bag and a revamp of the Scottish League on the way, there were two vacancies in the Third Division approaching, and Hector McLennan, the then chairman, sought Wilson's thoughts about applying for one of those places.

'I urged him to jump at the chance,' said Wilson. 'I always felt there should have been something for the club that won the Highland League every season, like access to a competition. But at that time, the reward was a financial one of around £1,200 to the champions. That was less than I received as a bonus for winning the title.'

The Staggies had impressed Scottish football by beating Queen of the

The Ross County squad that won the Highland League title in 1991–92.

(Back left–right):
Bobby Wilson (manager),
Davie Hamilton,
Jamie MacPherson,
Sandy Macleod,
Johnston Bellshaw,
Albert Allan,
Mike Ure,
Steve Hutchison,
Robert Allan,
Scott Lemon,
Brian Grant,
Don Cowie,
Chic Ogilvie.

(Front left–right):
Robbie Williamson,
Barry Wilson,
Chris Somerville,
Gordon Connelly,
Cameron Robertson,
Andy Macleod,
Alan Duff,
Gary Campbell,
Billy Ferries.

South 6–2 in the Scottish Cup, having drawn 2–2 with them at home. Players like Brian Grant, formerly of Arbroath, and Alan Duff, who had played with Inverness Caley, had impressed. So, too, had the manager's son, Barry, beginning to come through as a teenager, and who was to become one of the club's best players and perform at the highest level with Livingston and Inverness Caledonian Thistle in the Scottish Premier League.

It was a Scottish Cup trip to Forfar Athletic on 8 January 1994 that helped County gain entry to the SFL for the beginning of the following season. A famous victory was achieved after the intervention of Dundee United manager, Jim McLean, and the loan of the Arabs' footwear.

'There was snow and ice in Dingwall when we left for Forfar,' said Bobby Wilson. 'I called their chairman to check on ground conditions in Angus and was told the pitch was perfectly playable.

'We travelled down on the Saturday morning and it seemed to me that the conditions were not improving. When we reached the Swallow Hotel in Dundee, where we had booked lunch, I contacted our opponents again and, as the players lunched, David Roan, one of our directors, and I drove to Forfar to inspect the Station Park pitch. It was playable but brick hard, a pitch for multi-studded boots. We had none. We had a problem.

'In desperation, I called Jim McLean, whose team were playing away to Hearts. I asked him if we could borrow moulded-soled boots from him. He told us to gather the sizes we needed and to head for Tannadice and pick up the boots.

'We went on to beat Forfar 4–0 with Dundee United's footwear. It was a tremendous result, and one we might not have achieved had it not been for Jim McLean's help. Forfar had a player sent off after three minutes, but I don't think the result would have been different had they had 11 men on the pitch. Brian Grant hit a hat-trick and Barry grabbed the fourth. It was a great day.

'The following week, we had the vote for the teams who were to be admitted to the Scottish League. Our presentation, made by Hector and Donnie MacBean, the club secretary, was not as sophisticated as those of other applicants, with their pipers playing outside and video shows to the committee. Ours was fine-tuned on the train to Glasgow. But it was honest and sincere, with our representatives highlighting the good things we would bring to the Scottish Football League.

'We also needed a member club to second our application, and up stepped Forfar to do the honours, and along with Inverness Caledonian Thistle, Ross County were admitted.'

Wilson left the club in 1996 and has many fond memories of his time in charge. Under him, County embraced the higher level of football immediately and, with a strengthened team, won the Third Division championship in 1998–99.

They rose up the Second Division in impressive style, finishing third and, by dint of league reconstruction to allow for a 12-team Premier League, they were promoted to the First Division. Since then, they have continued to evolve, despite a blip that took them temporarily back to the Second Division.

THE MILLIONAIRE
AND THE CELTIC STAR

Another Wilson who made a huge impression at Victoria Park was Sammy.

Sandy Wallace was one of his disciples. Wallace was a rugby player transformed into an attacking right-back as Wilson encouraged stylish, attacking football during his time in charge at County.

Sammy, curly-haired and charismatic, had known prominence as a member of Celtic's League Cup-winning side of 1957, when the Hoops dismantled their great rivals Rangers in a 7–1 win. Wilson, picked up by Celtic on a free transfer from St Mirren in the spring of that year, was a hard-working inside-left and scored the opening goal that October day, while Billy McPhail, with whom he formed a formidable partnership, hitting a hat-trick.

Two years later, with McPhail having retired because of a knee injury, Wilson moved to Millwall. During his time at Celtic, he had combined playing with working as a motor mechanic – he had to work one Sunday in four to compensate for his absences on football business – but scored 46 goals in 70 appearances, a ratio any modern-day manager would love to have from a midfield player.

His move to Dingwall in 1962, persuaded to join County by Frank Thomson, the inspirational boss of Invergordon Distillers, and given a house and job in the distillery, came a year after the club couldn't enter the Scottish Cup because their 10s 6d (55p) wasn't paid.

Wallace, who played under Wilson, still holds the man who became his mentor in the highest regard.

'Thomson did the right thing in recruiting Sammy,' Sandy Wallace attested. 'Sammy was interested in the football development aspect of the club.

'I had been playing rugby at the time and I burst my shoulder so was trying to get myself fit and Sammy was coaching a bunch of guys in Invergordon, where he lived. I was gallus enough to go over and ask if I could join in.

'I had a little football trick I did, he liked it and invited me to the football club. I had gone to Robert Gordon's College in Aberdeen, a rugby-playing school, and here I was at 22 years old and with no background in football, turning to the round ball.'

Wilson's coaching and his love of the game rubbed off on the young Aberdonian who had migrated north to work on a salmon research scheme at Contin, Ross-shire. Sandy Wallace later became an industrial chemist at the Invergordon distillery, courtesy of Thomson. On the training ground, he was a quick and ready learner.

'I was a winger, but played a few games at centre forward,' he said, 'and it

took me about a year to get into the first team.

'Sammy was picking up guys all over the place to re-build the team, and he saw that I didn't have the turning skills as a winger. So, he made me into a full-back. In fact, Colin Brett, the left-back, and I were probably the first attacking full-backs in the Highland League. Colin was a failed inside forward, but found his niche at full-back.

'That's how I got into the team, because Sammy was a wonderful coach. Before him, County were very ordinary. Sammy changed all that. He changed the thinking and the ethos. Indeed, I believe he changed how north football thought.'

It was as Wilson prepared to push for the Highland League title that he wanted to augment the local lads in the team with bigger-name players with experience at a higher level. It was to prove a masterstroke and, backed by Thomson, players of the calibre of Jack Lornie, an Aberdeen forward who had performed for Leicester City in the FA Cup final in 1961 and subsequently played at Luton Town, Carlisle United, Tranmere Rovers, were brought on board.

It helped that Thomson was able to offer some of them employment at his distillery, and other players followed.

'We didn't get paid a lot,' says Sandy Wallace. 'My first wage was £1.10/-

(£1.50) a week while the inside forwards received £4 because, well, because they were inside forwards. That's just the way it was.'

A broken leg sidelined Sandy for 15 months, which meant that he missed the famous Scottish Cup tie against Rangers in 1966. The game had been scheduled for Saturday 12 February, but a waterlogged pitch caused its postponement for a week, although that game, too, had to be put back and the tie was eventually played on the afternoon of Monday 28th, but only after a monumental effort from club management and supporters in removing 18 inches of snow from the soggy Victoria Park playing surface.

Previewing the tie scheduled for 19 February 1966, when it was postponed for the second time, the *Scottish Daily Express* sportswriter John Mackenzie, dubbed 'the Voice of Football', described the scene at Victoria Park: 'I stood on the football pitch at Dingwall yesterday, where Rangers will play on Saturday.

'There were deep ruts and high ridges. The recent pictures of the moon suggested it might provide a better playing surface. First Division sides would have raised their hands in horror at Ross County's methods of making it fit for football.'

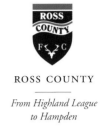

ROSS COUNTY

From Highland League to Hampden

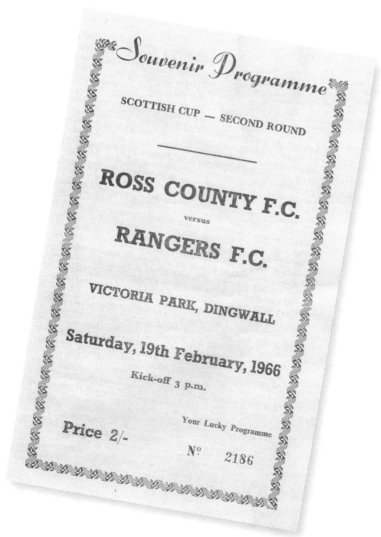

Souvenir Programme

SCOTTISH CUP — SECOND ROUND

ROSS COUNTY F.C.

versus

RANGERS F.C.

VICTORIA PARK, DINGWALL

Saturday, 19th February, 1966

Kick-off 3 p.m.

Price 2/-

Your Lucky Programme

N° 2186

Opposite.
Sammy Wilson is pictured second from the left in the front row of this County team which beat Inverness Caledonian at Telford Street in January 1962. The team also recorded a famous Scottish Cup win that season by beating Dumbarton 3–2 at Boghead with goals from B. Urquhart, E. Wilson and D. Oates. The County team is (Back left–right): Duncan, Greig, Anderson, McGilivray, Young, Urquhart.
(Front left–right): Chalmers, S. Wilson, Oates, Mackenzie, E Wilson.

Left.
The programme from the twice-postponed Scottish Cup-tie against Rangers.

Photographs showed a pitch churned up as if it had been subjected to a tractor-racing contest, although Mackenzie wrote of a 'great levelling job' and a two-inch dressing of top soil and sand to 'make it an excellent playing surface'. Unfortunately, it wasn't good enough and the game fell foul of the conditions.

In addition, Frank Thomson had ordered the laying down of peat moss, sand and leaf mould, brought in by lorries from local distilleries, to absorb the excess water. There was a determination that the tie should be played, although Rangers were known to be unhappy at such a decision with conditions overhead and underfoot making life difficult for the players. It was third time lucky, and 28 February was the big day, although it did not take place without a hitch or two.

Rangers had protested to the referee, J. Barclay of Kirkcaldy, that the pitch was unplayable. He disagreed and repeated his verdict an hour-and-a-half before the kick-off as the visitors insisted he carry out another inspection.

In the *Scotsman* of 1 March, Ron McKinnon, the Ibrox centre-half, was quoted as saying: 'This is the worst pitch I have ever seen.' A Rangers spokesman said: 'We couldn't risk Willie Henderson [their star winger] on that pitch.'

On his second inspection, the referee donned shorts, jersey and boots and took to the field with a ball. On one of his sprints, he fell over and landed flat on his face. A moment or two later, he declared the game on.

Frank Thomson fuelled the controversy by claiming it was Rangers' 'dictatorship' that led to the second inspection.

The Ross County team that day was:

Benny Sutherland (goalkeeper), a 32-year-old electrician from Muir of Ord who had been in the Highland League for 15 years; **Peter Borley** (right-back) 19 and a laboratory technician at the Invergordon distillery; **Colin Brett** (left-back) just 18 years old and a Dingwall Hydro Board worker who had made his debut the previous season; **Ian McNeill** (right-half) 33, a draughtsman at the distillery who had, by then, played for Aberdeen, Leicester City, Southend United and Dover Town; **Ian Greig** (centre-half) 25, computer programmer at the distillery. Previously rejected a chance to join Rangers; **Don MacMillan** (left-half), a 28-year-old former Celtic and Aberdeen signing noted for his rocket shot; **Tommy 'Tucker' Thomson** (outside-right), 24, a filling store gunman at the distillery who'd been at Inverness Thistle prior to joining County; **Sandy MacKenzie** (inside-right), 25. Eight years with the Staggies. An assistant warehouse manager at the distillery; **Denis Donald** (centre-forward), 21 and an Aberdeen signing in 1961, released two years later, and re-joined County five weeks before the Rangers tie; **Jim Hosie** (inside-left) County's top scorer, aged 27, another distillery employee; **John MacKay** (outside-left), 18, and taking an arts degree at Aberdeen University.

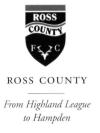

County versus Caley on 13 August 1960. Cathel Melville and Jimmy Davidson in an aerial challenge.
(*Dingwall Museum*)

ROSS COUNTY

*From Highland League
to Hampden*

The Rangers line-up, peppered with international players, was: Ritchie; Johansen, Provan; Watson, McKinnon, Greig; Wilson, Sorensen, Forrest, McLean, Johnston.

It appeared an insurmountable task for County against a side packed with stars of the quality of McKinnon, John Greig, Davie Wilson and Willie Johnston. It was therefore no surprise that the Ibrox team won through to the next round with a 2–0 victory, the goals coming from Johnston, then just 18, and George McLean.

The *Scotsman* described the action thus: 'When County forced three corners within the first three minutes, it was a pattern for things to come. For even Rangers will admit that in the following 87 minutes, this non-league side gave them one of the biggest frights they have ever experienced.

'The two goals that saw Rangers through came in the 25th and 26th minutes. The first was a drive to the far post by left-winger Johnston, which seemed to catch County keeper Sutherland on the wrong foot.

'The second was a scissors move between Forrest and McLean, which ended with the big inside-left shooting home from 12 yards.'

It is a cup tie that is still high on the list of great occasions in County's history and is featured elsewhere in this book, as some of those who turned out in the white strip they wore on that occasion re-tell their stories of the day Rangers came to town.

Interestingly, each match programme, which cost two shillings (10p), was numbered with prizes awarded to winners of the half-time draw. There were just five prizes, including a keg of salt herring and a bag of oatmeal, an indication, perhaps, of less sophisticated times.

The following year, by which time England had lifted the World Cup on home soil, Sandie Shaw's 'Puppet on a String' had won the Eurovision Song Contest for the UK and Jeremy Thorpe had succeeded Jo Grimond as leader of the Liberal Party, Sandy Wallace was in the County side and part of the team that won the Highland League for the first time in its history. The title was achieved with three games remaining.

Wilson had quit as manager in September 1966 to devote time to the hotel of which he was joint proprietor in Tain, and Ian McNeill was appointed player-coach. He was determined to become the first County boss to lift the Highland League title, albeit with Wilson's squad.

These were changing times. The Rolling Stones were having their '19th Nervous Breakdown' and Scott's Travel Agency in Dundee and Rutherglen advertised 15-day all-inclusive holidays in Majorca for a little over £76. James Stewart and Rock Hudson were starring in *Where the River Bends*, showing at the Dingwall Picture House.

County's surge in 1967 was part of that 1960s revolution, as they hoped soon after to edge their way into Third Division football. They would have to wait almost 30 years, however, to realise that ambition.

'Ian Greig played centre-half in those days,' said Sandy Wallace. 'Don MacMillan, a former Celtic and Aberdeen player was also in the team. He played left-half, a midfielder in today's terms. He was 6ft 2in tall and was a classic footballer with lovely balance.

'Jim Hosie, formerly of Aberdeen and Barnsley, was wonderful on the ball, and, of course, Jack Lornie was there too. We also had Ian Davidson, a tough-tackling inside-forward who had come from Aberdeen, as well as John MacKay, a local lad who could have gone senior but went off to university instead.'

McNeill did what he had set out to do, and in 1967 the league championship trophy sat in the Victoria Park boardroom for the first time.

Sandy Wallace's career at the club limped to a close when he suffered a cartilage problem at a time when treatment for such an injury was slow and tortuous. When he regained his fitness, he went to Wilson, by then coaching kids in the area, and he was keen to become involved.

'Sammy sent me to Largs to do an SFA coaching course, which I did alongside Alex Ferguson among other well-known figures in the Scottish game.

'I got a job at Ross County and coached the second team for a couple of years before moving to Inverness Clachnacuddin as manager in 1972.

'I spent three years there, winning the Highland League championship and the Qualifying Cup in my final year.'

Sandy returned to business and, around 1984, was invited back to County as manager. There was no money and the brief was that he should start from scratch, building a team from the surrounding area.

It was a task that appealed to him. He set up a coaching system and was manager at Victoria Park for three years.

But what of the Highland League in the twenty-first century?

'When I played, and after that, the league was good,' he insisted, 'because we had some strong clubs, like Inverness Caledonian and Elgin City. Caley always had money and therefore had a good team.

'Ross County became a good team, largely because of Frank Thomson, who generated money. From the mid-sixties onwards, they were considered a top Highland League team who always gave league opposition a good game in the cup tournaments, often beating them, as did Caley, Elgin, Keith and Peterhead. A lot of those teams are now out of the Highland League, which is weaker as a result. And, of course, it isn't as Highland as it used to be.

'Despite all the coaching and all of the effort, it isn't as easy these days to go and pick someone out and put them into the Highland League. It just doesn't work; to find players from a lower level and pitch them into the intense game we now have at Ross County is almost impossible. The standard of football at Victoria Park today is wonderful.

'When I sometimes look in on the squad training, I am amazed at the high intensity of it. Stunning stuff from high-quality footballers, and it's like that throughout most of the First Division. The standard is much higher, people are better on the ball, everything is quicker, the passing is crisper; it's different class.'

Sandy Wallace harbours fond memories of his days as a Ross County player and later as manager, but points to Bobby Wilson, his successor, as a coach who took the club to a new level.

ROSS COUNTY

From Highland League to Hampden

LUNCH WITH FREUD
AT THE NATIONAL HOTEL

Tommy Thomson's chest almost burst with pride when the club for whom he starred in their first Highland League championship-winning side in 1967 battled their way to the Scottish Cup final 43 years later.

The man who grew up with the nickname Tucker – 'I was given that name at school because my granny used to turn up at the school gates every morning at 10 o'clock and give me a cake' – is still revered by Ross County supporters of a certain age who remember his dazzling runs as a right winger, always keen to take on the full-back.

But his career almost stuttered to a halt before he made his way to the Dingwall club when a move to Third Lanark and a higher grade of football ground to a standstill after a fortnight.

'I was born in Inverness where I had played with Thistle from the age of 17 in the Highland League,' he said, 'and I was invited to go to Third Lanark. I was delighted, of course, but after being there just two weeks the signs were clear that the club was heading for extinction. I was very disappointed, but came back north and joined Ross County.

'Hugh Urquhart, the secretary of Ross County, signed me for the club and Frank Thomson gave me a job at his distillery.

'I was 23 when I signed. The team had Hosie, McNeill and MacMillan and they knew how to put the ball inside the full-back for me and they taught us all the tricks on how to distract defenders and beat them.'

Tucker was one of an army of admirers of Sammy Wilson and, like his team-mates, hung on his boss's every word, whether it was a mild, but private, chastisement for errors made, or comments of encouragement on how a winger could unpick defences with his pace.

Tucker Thomson was a key part of the side that faced Rangers in 1966 on that freezing February afternoon in the Scottish Cup second round. It was played on a Monday when, remarkably, County fans somehow found time to miss work commitments to be able to say: 'I was there.'

When, on 12 February, the tie was postponed for the first time, Frank Thomson treated the team to a meal in the National Hotel, just a long throw-in away from Victoria Park. As they took their seats for lunch, Tucker found himself seated between George Young, the great Rangers and Scotland defender of the 1940s and 1950s, there to report on the game for the *People* newspaper, and a young journalist dispatched from London by his sport editor to write a colour piece on the Highland minnows' attempt to overcome one of the biggest fish in Scottish football waters.

It was reminiscent of the latter stages of the 2010 Scottish Cup run, when national newspaper writers gravitated north for their 'underdogs bid for glory' tales.

Young had also agreed to undertake another duty while in the area, and was a judge of the Miss Ross County beauty contest at an eve of cup-tie dance in the Pavilion Ballroom, Strathpeffer.

'The sportswriter I sat next to that afternoon worked for the *Sun*,' said Tucker Thomson. 'He was Clement Freud, later to become a TV chef, presenter, a Liberal Party Member of Parliament, a knight of the realm, and the face of those dog food commercials on television. He was extremely good company.'

Rangers manager Scott Symon (centre) looks on as officials decide the blizzard-hit Victoria Park is unplayable on 19 February 1967.

Freud arrived from London to report on the tie for the then broadsheet paper, before it was bought over by media mogul Rupert Murdoch. His words on the big game were amusing. He began by mentioning his longer than expected connection with the area.

'Since Saturday of the week before last,' he wrote in the *Sun* of 1 March, the day after the Scottish Cup tie, 'I have had a sort of hate relationship with Ross County Football Club.

'The game should have been played in Dingwall on 19 February. I was in attendance; so was a blizzard, 3 inches of snow and a referee to call off the match. I flew back to London. Thereafter, each day I phoned the editor of the *Dingwall North Star and Farmers Chronicle* for news of the rearranged fixture.

'We passed from calling each other sir to Christian name terms; we started

asking each other about our families. Last Thursday, I was at London Airport bound for the North when the game was abandoned a second time. On Sunday night, he telephoned and said that this time it was a cinch – Monday, 3pm.'

He reached Victoria Park at 11.30am on the day of the game and proclaimed: 'I've seen bigger cinches.'

Freud's report also gives an insight into the state of the pitch, while he criticised the referee for bowing to Rangers pressure for a second morning pitch inspection.

'Surrounded by lush green fields untouched by human hand,' he wrote, 'the Highland club's pitch, having received unlimited attention by hosts of volunteers, was a chocolate coloured morass covered with a thick overlay of treacle.

'At noon, there came the first breath of trouble. Mr Scott Symon, the Rangers manager, having personally inspected the ground, requested the referee take a second look. Technically he was right; the ground was unsuitable for a football match. Morally, his conduct was as indefensible as taking an lbw decision to the House of Lords.'

Freud described the referee's last inspection and his falling over, yet labelled Rangers' demands as an 'ill-mannered exhibition of power politics which had gained them nothing but the disrespect of 9,000 honourable Highlanders'.

He agreed that the visitors deserved their victory, despite 'their multitudinous mistakes and their unendearing pre-match behaviour', and no doubt he would have been pleased to leave the Arctic conditions behind and head for the milder climes of the Home Counties.

Also there in the National Hotel dining room that Saturday afternoon, again sent north by a newspaper editor keen to capture the occasion in colourful terms, was the *Observer's* man on a Highland assignment, a young Chris Brasher, who in 1956 won gold in the 3,000-metre steeplechase at the Melbourne Olympics and was to found the London Marathon.

A Rangers fan, Tucker Thomson came face to face with Davie Provan, a Scotland international and, at 6ft 3in tall, towering above him by about nine inches.

The little winger's guile and speed had the defender twisted inside and out as he struggled to cope with the trickery of Thomson. 'I would put the ball past him and beat him and tease him, telling him he was too slow,' he said.

'My mum and dad, my two sisters and my brother were at the game and it was the best day until Ross County beat Celtic in the Scottish Cup semi-final in 2010.'

With memorabilia on his mind, Tucker persuaded his immediate opponent to part with his Rangers shirt and proudly clasped his prize as he entered the changing room. With the Ibrox club's finances in mind, however, his personal trophy was snatched from him.

'The Rangers game was my proudest moment. I got Provan's No. 3 shirt and took it into the dressing room, only to be followed in by Scott Symon, the legendary Ibrox manager.

ROSS COUNTY

From Highland League to Hampden

Opposite.
Tommy 'Tucker' Thomson (left), goalkeeper Benny Sutherland, and full-back Peter Borley, are piped out on to the pitch as they prepare to face Rangers.

'He was furious all day because the game had gone on in such atrocious conditions, and raged that I had the jersey.

'He said: "Glasgow Rangers can't afford to throw strips away every week." He demanded the jersey back, and Ian McNeill approached me and invited me to return my, by then, cherished possession with a promise that I could keep my own top, part of the new County strip Frank Thomson had bought for the team for the occasion. I agreed, and I still have it today.'

Tucker remembers the sense of occasion that day and the electric atmosphere of appearing before a sea of 9,000 faces, crammed in to the small football ground.

'People made all sorts of excuses for being absent from work that afternoon. Actually, I had to work at the distillery in the morning, and I wasn't alone among the team to have to put in a half-day at work. One man, an Irishman who worked alongside me, told his gaffer at the distillery that he wasn't able to be at his job because his wife was having a baby. He was 58. Somebody phoned in for him.'

Those were the days of hard drinking in the Highland League, he admitted, particularly when teams played away from home, and ensured that on their return from a game a pub or two would be visited en route.

'Our team did everything together, including drinking. Nine of us had jobs at the distillery which meant that when we were having our tea breaks we would discuss football and tactics. It definitely helped team spirit that we worked together, lived in the same area, most of us in the same street in Invergordon, and socialised together.

'We'd often meet up in the City Hotel in Elgin with many of the Highland League players who were Aberdeen-based, and Frank Thomson would always be ready to buy the players drinks, especially if, as frequently happened, he took money off you during the poker games on the team bus. But I liked him. He was a scholar and a gentleman and great for Ross County.'

Tucker's five-year stay with the Staggies ended in 1968, when he left for Brora Rangers and a new job as a porter in Raigmore Hospital, Inverness. From there, he worked in the plaster room at a major hospital in Manchester, where over a long period in orthopaedics he would be responsible for putting on and removing 'stookies' from the legs of a long list of Manchester City players, from goalkeeper Joe Corrigan to talented performers like Jim Tolmie, the former Morton winger who was signed for City by Billy McNeill in 1983 from the Belgian side Lokeren, and David White. After 24 years there, he returned to Inverness and Raigmore Hospital.

'I look back on my time at County with fondness. And that day we played Rangers was brought home to me during the Co-operative Insurance Cup tie against Dundee United at Victoria Park in season 2009–10.

'At half-time, I was asked to go to the main stand to meet someone. A Dundee man, now living and working in Inverness, greeted me and told me he'd been taken by his parents, all the way from Tayside, to support us against Rangers. He wanted to shake my hand and it was lovely to meet him. It was a true indication of the love people have of that wonderful Highland football club.'

ROSS COUNTY

From Highland League to Hampden

Tommy 'Tucker' Thomson holds the Scottish Cup with other County legends. Clockwise: Alan Duff, Robbie Williamson and Billy Ferries.
(*Material Marketing & Communications*).

INTO THE SFL WITH
HIGHLAND INTEGRITY

Scottish football was set to undergo a significant change for the start of season 1994–95. Rangers had finished the previous term as champions of a 12-club SPL, with Aberdeen runners-up, Motherwell third and Celtic taking fourth place.

Below that league, there were only the First and Second Divisions, and it was decided there would now be four leagues of ten teams, with the new clubs entering the Third Division.

This was Ross County's big moment and they threw their hat into the ring along with the merged Inverness clubs, Caledonian and Thistle. Elgin City and Gala Fairydean also applied.

Forrest Gump and *Pulp Fiction* had hit the cinemas, *Men Behaving Badly* was enjoying huge ratings on TV and David Dimbleby had just taken over from Robin Day as the host of BBC One's *Question Time*.

But while County's lobbying efforts moved into overdrive, there were some within the Scottish football hierarchy who thought that Dingwall was too small and too remote to sustain league football.

There was a determination, however, that a bid should be made to move out of the Highland League, having won two successive championships under manager Bobby Wilson, and join the bigger boys.

Club chairman Hector MacLennan and the secretary, Donnie MacBean, were the Dingwall envoys dispatched at the beginning of 1994 to make the case that County deserved to gain entry to the Scottish Football League. Secretly though, as it was widely expected that the Inverness application would be accepted, there was a feeling that other members of the SFL might take the view that having two outfits from the Highlands was a step too far.

Donnie, who remains secretary at Victoria Park, recalled how two nervous ambassadors took the train to Glasgow for the crucial gathering of the leading lights in the game and walked from Queen Street Station to the SFA headquarters at Park Gardens for the big showdown.

'When we arrived, there was a piper playing in front of the building to herald Gala Fairydean's application,' he said, 'and they had sent all the members videos of what their team would bring to league football. They used the video in their presentation. Our presentation amounted to a four-page pamphlet, while Hector and I had scribbled down a few notes as cue cards on the train.

'Gala even had Gavin Hastings, the Scottish international rugby star, there as a kind of special representative of the Borders town. His message was that Gala was more than just a rugby town.

Opposite.
Happy days in the Highland League when Fred Newton, later to become chairman, kept goal.

(Back left–right):
Colin MacLean, trainer,
George Sutherland,
Willie Urquhart,
Fred Newton,
Jimmy Farmer,
Finlay Browning,
Fred Nimmo,
Cecil MacIntyre (Chairman)

(Front left–right):
Chic Ogilvie,
Frank Simpson,
John Patience, Alex Ferguson,
Tommy Urquhart.
Ball boy Eck Wilson.
The team played in colours of primrose and blue.
(*Dingwall Museum*)

'I told them we had taken in players like Hosie, Lornie and MacMillan. Then I said, "Probably most of you will remember the name Sammy Wilson, and apologies to Campbell Ogilvie [the Rangers delegate] but he played for Celtic in the 7–1 defeat of Rangers in the League Cup final in 1957." That brought a few chuckles from some of those in the room.'

Donnie explained how influential Sammy had been when he arrived at Victoria Park as the manager when County were still in the Highland League, and how he had attracted players from outside the immediate area and produced attractive football.

'We just told them exactly what we were about and then we answered questions, though for a few nervous moments, nobody asked any. I told them we would go into the league as Ross County and wouldn't, as Ferranti Thistle had done by becoming Meadowbank, change our name. I told them there was room for two Highland teams to be there.

'The representative from East Fife spoke of finances and how he believed there was "loads of money floating about the Highlands", a reference to grants and the like from Highlands and Islands Enterprise. "Would you get any of that?" he asked.

'I said that if there was any cash floating around we'd certainly stretch up

ROSS COUNTY

From Highland League to Hampden

and try and grab some. There was money at that time but, while we received a certain amount, it didn't come as easily as many expected.

'Hector and I took a taxi to Queen Street Station and had a McDonald's, though knowing we'd be hungry later, Hector called his son, who worked in a chip shop in Aviemore, and when the train stopped there, chips were handed to us from the platform.

'We'd had no indication from the meeting whether we would be accepted, and it was a couple of months later when we were told. The voting system they employed wasn't one club, one vote. I think we got through on the second ballot. The whole event was nerve-wracking.'

Donnie's association with Ross County began in 1966 when he was a 16-year-old Air Cadet in Dingwall. Fred Newton, then the football club's chairman, arrived at a gathering of the Cadets one night looking for volunteers to sell programmes at County's second round Scottish Cup tie against Rangers.

'The programme sellers were given a special place under the BBC gantry, where we could watch the game after we'd sold all our allocation. It was a great night. There were 9,000 spectators there and the atmosphere was electric.

'That game started an association with Ross County which was built-up through the supporters' club, the development club and the social club, of which I became chairman.'

Going into the 2010 Scottish Cup final, Donnie, who worked for BT for almost 38 years – 17 as an area manager – had been club secretary for 28 years. Born and raised in Dingwall, his contribution to Ross County could not be understated.

'I think back to those days when Bobby Wilson was manager,' he said. 'He also worked on the club lottery, which paid his wages. We had 1,000 members paying £54 a year each. We gave out about half of it in prizes and for the first year anyone who was a member got into the games free and that made a big difference to the attendances. They went up to 800 or 900 at every home game.

'We had an incentive bonus for the players. Bonus payments were about £8 while they were on wages of £4. They were a good bunch of players in those days and, when we needed their help, the people of Dingwall have always rallied over the years by putting in money. Even going back to Frank Thomson's time running the club, when he changed it to a limited company, they always put their hands in their pockets. I remember we had a big response when we sold shares at £1 each. There were other appeals, like when we needed to upgrade the floodlights and we had our "Save Our Staggies" barometer in town.

'But a club like ours needs an investor. Roy MacGregor is our sugar-daddy and I don't know what we would have done without him.'

No-one would argue with that summation. Yet, without dedicated people like Donnie MacBean, small clubs like Ross County would cease to exist.

FINE FARE FINANCES
ENERGY FORTUNE

There can't be too many tycoons who have made the leap from selling beans to securing multi-million-pound oil deals.

Roy MacGregor did it in spectacular style, seizing opportunities he helped create and underlining that business expertise built up in retail could be translated into any of industry and commerce's most demanding disciplines.

Born and raised in Invergordon, and with little enthusiasm to enter the supermarket business his father, Alistair, and his grandfather, Rod, ran in the town and in Alness, the young MacGregor was happy to escape the 4 o'clock starts on Saturday mornings as a youngster helping out in one of the stores, when business college in Aberdeen beckoned.

He had dipped his toe in the world of football in 1967–68 as a teenage midfielder under Sammy Wilson at Ross County, the team he supported, though played only once for the first team and not in a competitive match.

He also worked so hard at his golf game that he played off scratch. There was recognition, however, that, despite the hours of practice, he would never make it in the professional ranks. Neither had he the desire to reach for the top in that competitive sport.

His time at college and, through a placement while in Aberdeen, his insight into the oil and gas industry, lit a touch-paper that was to lead to an explosion of energy and passion and a belief that he had found the niche which hitherto had eluded him. But he would have to wait.

Back in Invergordon after taking his business management degree, MacGregor set about revolutionising the family superstores.

'I decided that, if I was going to be a retailer, I wasn't going to do it the traditional way,' he said.

'We had two big superstores, each 20,000 square feet, and we were competing and winning against the multiples before the days of ASDA, and when Tesco was just a wee firm.

'I went to Boston, in the US, and brought in the first scanning and back-office systems that kept tabs on the stock and automatically re-ordered through computer when it was required.

'Taking the price off the tin and replacing it with a barcode was also a major issue. It was all about trust. Four years before the multiples adopted that method, we did it in Alness and Invergordon, and they came and looked at us.

'It worked with an independent because the trust element between us and the customer had to be ultimate to allow us to remove the price from the tin. Nowadays we take it for granted. We pioneered those two systems.'

MacGregor's commercial and marketing skills had moved the business, started by his grandfather just before the Second World War, into a higher gear, but the constant niggling from James Gulliver, the Scots boss of the giant Fine Fare supermarket chain, who made several attempts to buy them out, came to a head over lunch in London.

Gulliver, born in Campbeltown, Argyll, was a big beast of the business world. He built three businesses and made himself millions of pounds in the process before launching the bid for the drinks company Distillers in 1985, the defining issue of his life.

Gulliver was a man of great ability. He was awarded a first class honours degree in mathematics and engineering at Glasgow University where his former tutor, Professor Hugh Sutherland, described him as one of the most outstanding pupils he had known.

The £1.9 billion bid for Distillers by Gulliver's company Argyll in 1985 was the biggest in British history. Distillers was the cornerstone of the Scottish commercial establishment, and Gulliver stalked it for two years before launching his attack. His analysis revealed that it was both undervalued and very poorly managed.

Gulliver eventually lost Distillers to Guinness who, it emerged, had engaged in wholesale cheating which brought about the imprisonment of three of their most senior executives.

MacGregor's Stores may have been smaller fish to fry in the period that pre-dated the great Guinness scandal, but they were important to a man bidding to expand the Fine Fare empire.

'I had been back in the family business about a decade,' Roy MacGregor recalled, 'and my father and I thought we'd at least listen to what Jimmy Gulliver had to say.' His utterances, it transpired, were blunt and to the point: 'You can either sell me your business or I'll come and take it.'

'I took it on the nose,' MacGregor said. 'But my father was a realist and a pragmatist and on the flight back to Inverness he explained that Gulliver was talking sense. He pointed out that if Fine Fare opened up beside us they would take 30 per cent of our business. Gulliver was simply giving us good advice, albeit with a touch of brawn.

'We decided to go ahead with the deal but retained ownership of the super-markets on a 25-year lease. They were part of a property company we had and those two supermarkets became Somerfield and then the Co-op.'

The Fine Fare deal was lucrative and, with the oil industry beginning to take off in his own backyard as rigs started moving into the Cromarty Firth, there were rich pickings for MacGregor as his entrepreneurial antennae twitched.

'It made me look at what else we could do,' he said. 'We rented a few properties to companies involved in the oil industry and I became dragged into it, began to understand it and got myself involved.'

MacGregor Energy was born in 1986 with the aim of servicing the big hitters in oil. The young company was involved with the first floating construction vessel in the North Sea for BP, in the mix of upgrading all the

Roy MacGregor and
his wife Morag.

major rigs, and doing business with the oil yards in Invergordon.

'I bought a company in Aberdeen,' MacGregor said, 'and developed a really good business, continuing our association with BP, and I was part of the think tank with that company when, in 1986–87, oil was at $6 a barrel and it was costing $12 to get it out.

'The thinking had to change and it was interesting to watch John Brown, the BP boss, bring about that change as he took them private. They reduced their list of contractors from about 150 to six and we were one of the half-dozen. The others were multi-nationals and we were a little operation from the Highlands.'

By 1997, MacGregor Energy, started from scratch eight years earlier, was turning over £50m.

'We were about to expand our business and take in some operator people to raise it to the next stage, a £100m turnover, when the private equity group 3i made me an offer I couldn't refuse. On top of that, I had a partner who had 25 per cent of the business and he wanted out.

'Three weeks after the first approach, the business was sold for £20m. I wasn't unhappy about that. I kept some of my Highland businesses which were in the group and dabbled in other things.'

Roy MacGregor was just 40-years old and sitting on a fortune. He tried to do nothing for a while, but although the body was willing, the brain wasn't.

Much of his energy was given to Ross County in his role as chairman, as he sought to establish the football club as the hub of the community of Dingwall and its environs.

Everything was to change in 2005, however, after learning that his oldest

son, Donald, a subsea engineer in Aberdeen, was set to move to Perth, Australia, with the company for whom he worked.

'The bottom line was that my wife Morag didn't want him to leave. We needed to prevent him from going to the other side of the world.

'So I said I'd start a wee business in Aberdeen to keep him here. On 7 January 2005, I opened it in a serviced office in Riverside Drive in the Granite City, thinking I'd have a £3m–£4m business involved in the subsea industry. I had a £1m overhead and no business; that focuses you.'

Five years later, Global Energy Group boasted 23 businesses, headquartered in Aberdeen, with a turnover of £240m and 3,500 employees, a sprinkling of whom are in far-flung places like Houston, Trinidad, Norway, Malta, Dubai and Cameroon.

MacGregor's recipe for success is to surround himself with those who know how to do their jobs well, motivate them and instil in them an important principle he learned all those years earlier in the retail trade: the customer is king.

'All I did was take that ethos to a different business,' he said, 'with a bit of common sense and smart people around me. We went back into a business we knew and one where the customer trusted us.'

Sons Donald and Iain are directors of the company while John, an accountant, is also on board. A fourth son, Ally, works in the company's Inverness offices.

Roy MacGregor believes implicitly in team-building within business. His empire has been built on such a platform and has its own in-house leadership scheme.

'It's the same motivation in football: if you improve people and give them a path, your business – your football team – will get better.

'That drives my business, making people better. If you get everybody on the bus with the same values and behaviours and traits, the business goes. If you have people on the bus who don't value what you believe in, you tell them they shouldn't be on the bus.'

In 2009, the *Sunday Times Rich List* put the MacGregor family fortune at £45m, a sum of money they would never have amassed selling beans.

ROSS COUNTY:
A TEAM FOR THE HIGHLANDS

It was 1977 and Roy MacGregor was persuaded by Gordon MacRae, chairman of Ross County FC, to join the board of the club. The new director was just 25 years old and keen to bring some fresh enthusiasm to the Highland League outfit.

After all, he had supported them since he was a schoolboy before signing for them as a callow youth of 16.

Like all clubs in the league at that time, County was a committee-driven organisation and, after six or seven years being smothered by that system, he quit his seat in the boardroom. But he returned after a few years, this time to effect the changes he believed were needed to take the club forward.

His energy, it was felt, might help County step up a level and apply for admission to the third tier of the Scottish Football League. MacGregor's talents in the art of lobbying were deployed, with his brief to persuade the chairmen of Premier League clubs that County deserved a place within the SFL scheme.

'Those clubs each had four votes in the system,' he said. 'I worked hard, but we were worried that, should Inverness Caledonian Thistle be admitted, the powers in Glasgow might see the admission of two Highland clubs as a step too far. Gala Fairydean were expected to win the second place up for grabs. Those Premier League votes would be key.

'The golden era of our Highland League championship win was on our curriculum vitae and, of course, we had that wonderful time under Bobby Wilson in the early 1990s, when we won two titles.

'Bobby had turned the club around and was the biggest influence, along with getting the strategy right, to us being admitted to the SFL.'

County's excellent Scottish Cup run the previous season had also been important in flagging-up that they were good enough to hold their own in the Third Division and, said MacGregor, despite a 'no' vote from Dundee United and Rangers, their application was rubber-stamped.

'The member clubs liked our business plan and to pick two teams from the Highlands was exceptional. I was privileged to be involved in that.'

Moving into the chairman's seat a year later brought with it a need for tough and uncomfortable decisions, one of which was to sack Wilson, a move which was not universally popular at the time. It certainly did not go down well with the manager, one of the club's most successful.

'I had a vision which was based on me wanting me to give every youngster an opportunity in our area to play football at a reasonable level, without them

having to leave,' said MacGregor. 'To do that, I knew we'd require a full-time team.

'We had gone into the league with a support of about 300–400 and we needed to have 2,000 fans at Victoria Park for every home game to be able to sustain a full-time squad.'

A revolution was underway and radical change effected with the introduction of 12 community officers, from Shetland to Oban. Quite simply, MacGregor sought to make Ross County the club of the Highlands, whether it was merely encouraging people to buy a £1 lottery ticket or attend a game once a year. In short, he wanted to recruit the citizens of the Highlands to become County supporters.

'We always knew football fans in Inverness would stick with their local team. However, surprisingly, 80 per cent of our corporate income comes out of Inverness and half our support is from the Highland capital.

'We needed to move the club on from where Bobby had taken us. He was a very successful Highland League manager and had done so well with little or no resources. He did a remarkable job. I just felt to take us to the next level required something different.'

MacGregor's decision to relieve Wilson of his post was seen by many as foolish, by others as bold and brave.

Alastair Kennedy was recruited to market County in the community and to edge the club towards being a proper business.

A former Highland league player with all of the Inverness teams who had turned down County in the Sammy Wilson–Sandy Wallace era, Kennedy had been head of business development at Highland and Islands Enterprise, a businessman with knowledge of football.

He brought corporate money into the club through hospitality packages and sponsorship, and wealthy business people came on board as sponsors, putting hundreds of thousands of pounds into the club's coffers.

Men like Tom Mackenzie, Alistair Matheson, Ronnie Fraser, Pat Munro and others were overwhelmingly generous.

Kennedy was appointed chief executive, a job he later relinquished, and took a seat on the board, where he remains.

Neale Cooper, finishing his playing career at Dunfermline Athletic after a glittering life in football as a multi-medal winning member of Alex Ferguson's all-conquering side of the 1980s, then with Aston Villa and Rangers, answered MacGregor's call: 'How would you like to take on your first management job at Ross County?'

The chairman wanted a different type of team boss from Bobby Wilson. He called for the kind of drive and aggressive style the rookie manager could bring to Victoria Park, where he could put in place the kind of good practice he had learned under Ferguson and at Rangers, where Graeme Souness was in charge.

'Neale gave us a dynamic that got us started and we went a couple of years as a part-time team, then we took in three full-time players, then five, and so it built up.

'Kenny Gilbert, who had been with Aberdeen in his early days, arrived from Hull City; Roy McBain, now with Inverness Caley, joined us from Dundee United; and Gerry Farrell, a player Neale knew from Dunfermline, were the full-time pioneers.

'We wanted young guys of 19 or 20 who were on the fringe of the first teams wherever they played but who weren't good enough for those sides. They trained during the day with Neale and then again at night with the part-timers. They stayed in a cottage in the Black Isle and at one time there were seven of them in there.'

But why put money into a football club where there would be no financial return? The importance of investing in the area in which he was born and raised proved too important for Roy MacGregor to be ignored. Football was a vehicle through which he could do his bit for his own community.

'The people who put money into football clubs come and go. If someone puts cash into a club for ego or pride or for what they can get out of it, it will go bump.

'I wanted to give something back to an area which gave me my livelihood, and football is one of the mechanisms for doing that. If you are successful, you have to give back.

'I also wanted to create opportunities for fellow Highlanders because this part of the world is in my soul. Historically, it is an area that was persecuted. Some people may say it's still like that today. There are some first-class people in the Highlands, though most of our young people leave in search of success elsewhere and never return.

'Why couldn't we do something here? Sport was a method by which we could do it. I get my pride and my enjoyment in giving and my biggest joy from the Scottish Cup final on 15 May 2010 was looking at the 20,000 Ross County fans at Hampden, not the football match.'

Pouring cash into a local football club, however, was not enough for the business tycoon. He wanted something more meaningful, and his thoughts alighted on a massive community programme, through the auspices of the football club, to aid people from all walks of life.

Research was required and he set off on a mission of learning, seeking enlightenment and the flash of lightning that would show him what he might do to touch as many Highlanders as possible.

'I realised the football academy system was important, and in my desire to build the first academy in Scotland I went to England, where their system allowed clubs to take people only from an area within two hours' drive, hence the reason some of the big clubs have systems in place on the Continent.

'Their funding was not for capital expenditure but operational costs. That meant the clubs in England had to build their academies and then running costs were funded by the English FA.

'In Scotland, the government was at that stage willing to fund the building of academies but the clubs had to find the operational money.'

MacGregor looked at academies in some of the main cities in England, and one or two of the provincial clubs and eventually saw two superb models, at

ROSS COUNTY
_____

From Highland League to Hampden

Norwich City and at Ipswich Town. It was the latter that inspired him.

'The Ipswich Town chairman, David Sheepshanks, explained how, despite being a provincial club with a catchment area of 200,000 people, they could attract 25,000 gates to Portman Road.

'He showed me a community complex behind one of the stands which had 72 community coaches, only six of whom were employed by the club.

'There were teachers, social workers, policemen and all sorts of people put into the club by their own organisations to influence the community and deal with some of the difficult and more pressing social aspects of the town.

'They were using the football club brand and Ipswich Town was benefiting by having one in eight of the population buying-in to this and becoming automatic supporters. This blew my mind.

'So, I returned and did a deal with the Scottish government to do something similar at Dingwall and for a time we received £500,000 a year to develop a plan to tackle some of the social problems in the area through football.

'This went on for six years. If Ipswich could get 12 per cent of the population in through their doors, I thought, how could I touch the 100,000 people in our area? The answer was that I had to give something and then I would get something in return.'

The die was cast. Personnel from Job Centre Plus, from the teaching profession, social work and the police were among those seconded to Ross County's life-skills team, using the football club brand to help the people of the area. County's strap line – more than just a football team – came from that initiative.

'We had a programme involving primary seven children going to a secondary school in a remote area six weeks before the end of term. We took them to the football academy and gave them football coaching. We also gave them an hour of physical activity in the secondary school they were to move up to the following term.

'It was a way for them to bond with their new school, and a simple thing like that identified all manner of problems, from child abuse to drug use and other difficulties, from the home lives of some of those children, problems of which the school was unaware.

'We got to understand all this by taking them away from their environment and engaging with them and it afforded the secondary school so much information about what they were getting.'

Invigorated by the success of the various programmes instigated by the club, Roy MacGregor is happy to cite a catalogue of examples of how they worked before funding halted.

'We were challenged by the Job Centre to deal with people who had been receiving benefits for more than ten years and there was this man who had been 19 years on benefits.

'The authorities had tried everything to get him into a job, but he would hardly ever leave the house.

'How do we get him out? We sat down with him over two or three weeks

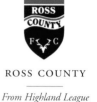

ROSS COUNTY

From Highland League to Hampden

A hen night with a difference for a bride-to-be County fan and her colourful friends gathering outside Hampden for the cup final. *(Ken Macpherson)*

31

and eventually he agreed to go with us to the football club where we branded him; we kitted him out in Ross County tracksuit and the like.

'We involved him in a mixture of individual and team sports of which football was just a part. There was classroom stuff, too. All we were doing was allowing him to recognise he could rediscover his self-esteem. After ten weeks he got a job in a supermarket and within three months he was appointed an under-manager there. And all that after being stuck in the house for 19 years.'

There are countless other examples of how Ross County changed peoples' lives and underlined the power of the club's brand when other agencies had little or no influence.

Goodwill, borne out of being seen to be injecting something significant into the local community, brought a new wave of supporters. But it was not all about encouraging people through the Victoria Park turnstiles, it was about how the club could put its stamp on the community.

Neale Cooper's six-year stay ended in 2002, and with the building of the football academy it was thought that hiring Alex Smith, one of the most experienced coaches in the Scottish game, was the way ahead. It was the right decision for the academy, MacGregor insisted, but the wrong one for the football squad.

'It was wrong because Alex was two generations away from the players, their thinking, their modus operandi and their attitude. He was 65, and while we respected the technical knowledge Alex had, the personal relationships between him and the players were too far apart.

'Alex's contract was up for renewal and we decided against offering him a new one. He took it badly. The team was doing relatively okay and he finished fourth or fifth each season.

'It was a hard thing to do, but it was right. When you're in a leadership role it isn't easy to tell people you have to move on without them.'

The manager's chair was then offered to John Robertson, a legendary striker with Heart of Midlothian who had taken Inverness Caledonian Thistle into the SPL in 2004 before returning to Tynecastle as head coach. He took Hearts to two cup semi-finals, enjoyed a reasonable run in Europe and finished fifth in the league, none of which saved him from the sack in May 2005, prompting County to recruit him. It was at a time when MacGregor, keen to devote more time to his embryonic business, handed over the reins of the club to friend and colleague Peter Swanson.

The Robertso–Swanson marriage was not one made in heaven, and a clash of personalities, brought to a head over the playing budget, prompted the departure of the manager, after just four months.

MacGregor was disappointed it had ended badly, particularly as he felt the former Scotland striker could have won promotion that season.

Gardner Speirs took over as interim manager, but his contract was not renewed on the basis that it was felt that while he was an able No. 2, he did not have what County needed in a manager.

MacGregor returned as chairman in 2006 with the decision to appoint a young manager in the shape of Scott Leitch, the Motherwell captain, whose playing career was coming to a close.

'He worked hard at it but couldn't make the move from player-captain to manager,' was how the chairman viewed Leitch. 'He lasted a year and we were relegated on the last game of the season to Gretna. We slipped into the Second Division.'

Dick Campbell, who in an earlier life sported long flowing locks and as a young Ross County player was known as Richie, emerged as the new manager, one who had been turned down on three previous occasions.

Interestingly, Derek Adams then in the team and still only 32, was also an applicant, though was passed over for a more grizzly type of manager with a reputation for motivating players and winning promotion. He was, in the opinion of the board, a safe pair of hands.

With just eight games played, however, and the Staggies sitting at the top of the Second Division, the axe fell on the manager.

'I decided it wasn't right,' MacGregor said, 'that I had made a mistake in appointing him. His style of football was neither attractive nor entertaining. I realised I'd made an error and gave Derek the job.'

There was concern and criticism in equal measure from MacGregor over the future of our national game, a sport squeezed so tightly that the entertainment value was at its lowest level. Football required greater leadership, a ten-year plan, to lift it from the doldrums. It certainly did not need a few elite chairmen who put self-interest first.

He condemned clubs who had no interest in their fans other than wishing to relieve them of their money on a Saturday afternoon and keep them at arm's length.

'Our ethos is about making the lot of the people you represent better, and if you do that and people like what they see, they will come and buy.

'Within three years of being at Ross County, I was at Morton standing on the terracing with 1,500 people there. I thought: how does this function?

'It was a ground that held more than 20,000 people at the time and I'm looking out and everything was dead, but round about it was a former community that once had the shipyards and the pubs, all built round the football club. That was lost because they didn't talk to their customers, and football is still like that today. Until you do it, in whatever form, you'll never get back to being a successful football club.

'Everyone's the same but you have different roles within whatever it is you're trying to achieve. The man who saves his money and comes on the train from Kyle, has his pie and a pint in the pub, comes to Victoria Park, then saves his money to repeat that exercise two weeks later, is the same as me giving what I've got, albeit it in a more privileged way. We are each giving back to the same cause; there's no difference.

'They say it's money that's destroyed football. I think it's people on ego trips who've destroyed football and are in football for the wrong reasons, principally for what they can get out of it.'

Those are strong words which would have many administrators, chairmen and directors shifting uneasily in their boardroom seats. But listening to the views of George Adams, County's director of football, that the club must aim

ROSS COUNTY

From Highland League to Hampden

Martin Scott and Steven Craig, County's goal-scorers against Celtic, and two players whose careers faltered elsewhere. (*Ken Macpherson*)

higher, MacGregor agreed to temper his views over the 'community club' tag.

'I believe in community and in giving opportunity,' he said, 'but we're not going to be taken seriously until we're an SPL club. George was brought up in the Fergie arena, where there was a siege mentality and claims from the manager, perhaps for psychological reasons, that everybody in the central belt was against Aberdeen.

'I think you could do both. We'll certainly never ditch the community club label. It's just a question of emphasis. Derek and George Adams developed a football team which is very focused and socialist in how they are with each other. They've taken players who haven't succeeded elsewhere and have moulded them into a solid unit.'

MacGregor's admiration of the young team boss is well documented. Single-minded, is how he describes him. He recognised in the young Adams, when as a youngster he arrived from Burnley, that he had someone special on his hands; a 22-year-old boy with the head of a 35-year-old.

'I was given a sixth sense in business because of my family background. Derek was given that sixth sense because every day he discussed and thought

about football because of his father. He always wanted to be a coach. He's got there, but he's got a wonderful mentor in his dad. You can't buy that experience.'

It was in April 2009 that MacGregor stepped down as chairman and became club president. Dave Siegel, managing director of County's shirt sponsors, HIGHnet, an Inverness-based telecommunications provider, took on the role.

But it is the philanthropic nature of Roy MacGregor that marked him out as special to Ross County, and while bandying figures around was not his style, tales of his generosity are legend.

Could it have been true that he provided the £400,000-a-year it takes to run the football team?

Did he really put up the money to transport 2,000 primary schoolchildren from Dingwall and the surrounding area to that glorious cup final day in Glasgow?

Was it not he who subsidised the 100-plus buses which transported 8,000 County fans to the national stadium to cheer on their team against Dundee United?

Ross County fans celebrate after seeing their team beat Celtic in the Scottish Cup semi-final. (*Press & Journal*)

The Ross County end at Hampden. The anticipation builds for fans from the Highlands. (*Ken Macpherson*)

It is certainly known that 1,500 of his staff from Global Energy, a clutch of Highland Councillors, MSPs and MPs, not to mention former club heroes, and disadvantaged people from all over the region, were there courtesy of his willingness to dip into the wealth he amassed from Highland beginnings.

'I still fund the club,' he confirmed, 'and probably make most of the decisions. But the sums of money involved would probably frighten me if I totted them up. They'd certainly frighten my wife Morag.'

Roy MacGregor is philanthropic for the right reasons. If he couldn't afford it, he couldn't be so generous, was how he put it. Between the academy and the football ground, the club has spent about £8m or £9m, with £1m of debt, a deficit he describes as 'very reasonable'.

The Scottish Cup final would change Ross County forever, he believed. For the older generation, it was their climax. The club could not now go back.

'Six and seven-year-old kids supporting the club will grow up and expect cup finals to come about more often. Whatever the cost of having people enjoy such a momentous day as 15 May 2010, was irrelevant; it was a historical day for Ross County.'

McNEILL MAGIC
WORKS AT COUNTY

Ian McNeil had two spells at County, although he could probably challenge for a place in the *Guinness Book of Records* as a football man who had played, coached, managed, or scouted for more teams than any other person.

A small man with a big heart, once encapsulated in a newspaper headline as THE MIGHTY ATOM, Glasgow-born McNeill achieved legendary status at Ross County as the man who, when he was player-manager, guided them to that first-ever Highland League crown.

His time in football spanned an astonishing seven decades, starting in 1949 at Aberdeen where, his career interrupted by National Service, he was unable to make a breakthrough because of top-scoring Harry Yorston, who hit 98 goals in 201 appearances for the Dons.

But there was hope on the horizon and Davie Halliday, the Aberdeen manager who had moved to Leicester City as McNeill completed his military service in the Royal Air Force – he was stationed in Kenya for a time and turned out for their international side against Uganda – took him to Filbert Street.

And so began life as a football gypsy, with stopover camps at Brighton & Hove Albion, Southend United and Dover before he arrived at Dingwall for the first of two stays.

Signed by Sammy Wilson and given the almost obligatory job in the Invergordon distillery, McNeill's influence and experience as player-manager following the departure of team boss Sammy Wilson were important components in Ross County capturing their first Highland League title in 1967.

'We had so many good players in the side during that first spell,' he remembered. 'There was a great atmosphere at the club at that time, with lots of characters, like Tucker Thomson who, during that game against Rangers, a club for whom I would have loved to have signed, kept beating Davie Provan. Mind you, the Ibrox left-back chopped him down whenever he got close enough.

'There was a tremendous fuss over the state of the pitch that day, but the running joke about Jim Forrest, the Rangers centre-forward, was that he didn't even get his shorts dirty. At least that's what my nine-year-old son, Ian, who was a ball boy, told me that's what people in the crowd were saying.

'I was fortunate in that I more or less kept the same team throughout my first spell at County and that allowed us to knit as a unit.'

The path to that famous cup-tie started with a preliminary round against Forfar at Victoria Park on 22 January 1966. The *North Star* reported that 'County's Lapse Had Fans Worried'.

Ian McNeill in his days with Brighton & Hove Albion.

The Invergordon Distillery Pipe Band's pre-match entertainment had raised the spirits of the team and the crowd, and they raced to a two-goal lead, first through a Don MacMillan thunderbolt from 20 yards, then from Jim Hosie a minute later.

The excitement generated by those goals was tempered early in the second-half as the team from the Second Division battled back to 2–2, despite being down to ten men following the ordering off of a young player by the name of Archie Knox, whose over-zealous lunge at Tucker Thomson was heavily penalised.

Knox was later to emerge as the assistant manager to Alex Ferguson at Aberdeen and Manchester United, and to Walter Smith at Rangers. In addition, he held coaching posts at Millwall, Livingston and Bolton Wanderers, was manager of Dundee and took charge of the Scotland under-21 side for a time. Knox was appointed assistant manager to Craig Brown at Motherwell in 2010.

With the tension mounting in that tie against Forfar, McNeill grabbed a third goal while Thomson fired home the winner five minutes from the end to cancel the Angus club's goals scored by John Park (2) and their player-manager Doug Newlands.

It was a heroic win, a victory that less than 24 hours earlier, Ian McNeill thought he might not have been able to participate in.

'I had appeared on the Grampian Television programme *Sportscope* with Frank Thomson the previous evening,' he recalled. 'We were interviewed by Archie Glen, the former Aberdeen wing-half, but as Frank's chauffeur's drove us back north in the fierce wintry conditions, the Rolls skidded off the road in the Glens of Foudland in Aberdeenshire and trundled down an embankment and into a field.

'It was a nasty experience. We were badly shaken and I remember making several unsuccessful attempts to get back up the embankment, slithering down several times before eventually making it to the top. Thankfully, I was able to play against Forfar the following day but I felt sorry for the driver. All he could think was what Mr Thomson would say. Frank was fine about it.'

Another Scottish League side, Alloa Athletic, had to be disposed of, again in the depths of winter, which brought conditions that were to prove so problematic that the scheduled tie, in the first round proper, had to be postponed.

The call-off, however, did not come until the County fans had made their way south, many of them packed on to a special supporters' train which left Dingwall directly for Stirling.

It meant that the pubs of Stirling and the surrounding area were crammed with Highlanders who had time to kill until later that evening, when the return journey was scheduled.

Unsurprisingly, by the time the train arrived back in Dingwall in the wee small hours of the following morning, many Highlanders were rather the worse for wear.

The game at Recreation Park eventually took place on 11 February 1966, and what a thriller it was. Eight goals were scored, with County snatching five of them through a brace each from Denis Donald and Tucker Thomson, and one from John MacKay.

It was stunning display to set-up that lucrative tie with Rangers.

Ian McNeill was an inspirational member of the County side and an able coach and manager, qualities that were recognised by Wigan Athletic, then in the Northern Premier League, who lured him south as their manager in 1968. He was instrumental in manoeuvring them into league football south of the border and was associated with them later in his career.

One of his players at County, Dennis Laughton, was transferred to Morton with a clause, unusual in those days, that should he be sold on, the Staggies would receive a cut of the fee.

'Laughton went to Newcastle United,' said McNeill, 'but the deal involved a swap with a Newcastle player which wiped out the sell-on percentage. I think there were thoughts that we had been stitched up.'

Laughton was in good company at St James' Park in the 1970s. Alongside him in the first-team squad were the former Aberdeen player Jimmy Smith, Terry McDermott, later of Liverpool, and great Newcastle players Frank Clark and Malcolm MacDonald.

Interestingly, Laughton had scored an own goal when playing for Morton against the Tynesiders in a Texaco Cup-tie in Newcastle in October 1973, the game that had brought him to the attention of Joe Harvey, manager of the English club.

In his second period at Ross County – from 1971 to 1976 – and by now having given up playing, he led them to the Qualifying Cup for the first time and secured a North of Scotland Cup triumph, too. But there was one result in that second stint that gave him nightmares; a 10–1 defeat to Inverness Thistle.

'We had a really good left winger from Dundee called John Wilkie, whom I later took to Wigan Athletic,' McNeill said. 'He scored our goal that day against Thistle, and in the dressing room afterwards with heads down and demoralisation in the air, John nearly caused a riot.

'He pointed out he had done his job by scoring. He clearly thought he was not culpable in any way for this crushing and embarrassing defeat.'

McNeill's management, coaching and scouting skills brought him employment at leading clubs from Chelsea, where he was assistant manager under John Neil, then John Hollins, to scouting for Liverpool under Kenny Dalglish, and to being chief scout for Bolton Wanderers and Leeds United, his final port of call. He retired in 2006.

ROSS COUNTY

*From Highland League
to Hampden*

A GOTHENBURG
GREAT ARRIVES

With the departure of Bobby Wilson as manager in 1996, a sacking that was to sour relations between him and the club for many years – though time eventually healed the rift – thoughts turned to who could be found to revolutionise the playing side of the club, one with only three full-time players, all part of the government's YTS scheme.

Neale Cooper, a gifted Scotland youth player and a vital cog in Alex Ferguson's Aberdeen team before moving on to Aston Villa and Rangers, had just been released by Dunfermline, his career by then ravaged by injury.

Cooper's name is still synonymous with the Dons, though, as one of the stars of the side that beat Real Madrid in the final of the European Cup-Winners' Cup in the Ullevi Stadium in Gothenburg in 1983.

He was helping on the SFA coaching course at Largs in the summer of 1996 when he was tipped-off that County were searching for a new manager. It was suggested it would be a useful baptism for him, perhaps as a player-manager.

He applied, and during the interview, he recalled, it was made clear that the aim was for the then Third Division side to be playing First Division football within five years.

He was offered the job, but quickly found out two things: football management can damage your health, and that playing while also being the boss didn't work, at least not for him.

He suffered a disastrous start to his campaign – County lost their first six or seven games – and spent two days in hospital for treatment to an abscess in his throat.

'I already had a sore throat,' he said at the time, 'but continuing to scream my head off did nothing to help matters. I ended up in hospital with a drip feed and unable to eat or drink anything for two days.

'It is a stressful job and I can't stop shouting. But it's up to the players to keep me quiet. If I'm screaming at them it means I'm not happy.'

Putting himself in the Staggies line-up also had its downside. 'I found it impossible to be player-manager,' he said. 'I turned out for the team a few times in the early days, but it was a nightmare and didn't work for me. I took myself off during one game and somebody shouted, "Cooper, that's the best decision you've made." It's bad enough getting stick as the manager, but as a player as well… it's not good.'

The introduction of new recruits brought improvement and County began to haul themselves up the league table, just missing out on promotion

Kenny Gilbert: 'Best player I signed,' said Neale Cooper. (*Ken Macpherson*)

ROSS COUNTY

From Highland League to Hampden

that season. Kenny Gilbert, Steven Ferguson, Roy McBain and Gary Wood were among those added to the squad. Derek Adams also came in, but Cooper remembered that it was not always easy to persuade potential employees that their future lay in the Highlands.

'The hard thing was to attract players because of the geography of the place. If players were offered similar wages in the central belt they would take it rather than have to travel to the Highlands. That's why we had to give them a little more.

'But the big thing for us was to encourage them to have a look at the club, the ground, Dingwall, and the area. Once they did that they wanted to stay.'

Cooper wanted to strengthen his side and was keen to add taller players. He was informed that Hull had released the former Aberdeen midfielder and defender Kenny Gilbert and despite being disappointed on seeing that he was not as tall as he expected, Cooper insisted he was 'pound for pound the best signing I've ever made'.

He added: 'Kenny was tenacious and had a desire to do well. If I'd had 11 boys like him I would have been very happy. He might not have been the most gifted player, but he was so hungry and had a big heart.

'In fact, he played one season not only with a serious eye problem but also

Neale Cooper (front centre) with one of his squads. (Ken Macpherson)

42

with a hernia. He kept playing and collapsed after the last game of the season, went to hospital and had operations for each condition within a few days of each other.'

Cooper maintained good progress with a constant, some might say extensive, turnover of players, and he assembled a more than useful squad with what he described as a 'good bunch of boys' including Frenchman Franck Escalon in the middle of the pitch, Sandy Ross – 'a great signing for me' – Ian Maxwell and Derek Adams.

Stuart Golabek was also a key member of Cooper's squad, having joined County the previous year. He began his career in the Highland League with Clachnacuddin and moved to County in 1995. He made only 36 appearances in his four years at Victoria Park before establishing himself as a fine left-back at rivals, Inverness Caledonian Thistle, where he took part in that club's famous Scottish Cup win over Celtic at Parkhead on 8 February 2000, which precipitated the departure of the Glasgow club's management team of John Barnes, Eric Black and Kenny Dalglish, the director of football.

From 2007 Golabek, born in Inverness, shuttled between Caley Thistle and County, and he became Dick Campbell's first signing for the Dingwall club in May 2007 after being released. Two years later, however, he returned to the Caledonian Stadium under manager Terry Butcher in September 2009, by then at 35 years of age, in the twilight his career.

Neale Cooper achieved the promotions he sought and took County into the First Division a year ahead of schedule, but after six years in the job and with his team sitting low in the table, it was time for a parting of the ways.

'I remember when that time came,' he said. 'We were playing Caley Thistle at Victoria Park and I couldn't have worked harder in my preparation. Within a few minutes we were two goals down and at that point I knew I'd gone as far as I could with the team.

'We were walloped in the end. They were big and strong and we were poor, and after that game I was very low. I drove to Aberdeen to see my family and spent the Sunday thinking about what I should do. I came to the conclusion that I had done my spell at County and the following morning I drove north to meet with Roy MacGregor and told him how I felt, and that was that. I left.

'They appreciated what I'd done, and I think I revolutionised the club during my time there and did the job I'd been tasked to do: get them into the First Division.'

ROSS COUNTY

From Highland League to Hampden

STORIES FROM EX-STAGGIES

Camaraderie and fun are the principal elements that shine through when tales of Highland League football at Buckie or Brora, Cove or Clachnacuddin are recounted. Stories of drinking and questionable behaviour are legend across the Highland League, and one such piece of narrative saw Ross County at its centre.

It came during the period Morris Newton, a well-known local business-man, was chairman. His father, Fred, had been at the helm at Victoria Park before him.

It was said that before a Highland League Cup final against Inverness Caledonian at their ground, Morris, who ran the family garage and bus company at the time, arrived in the County dressing room and placed a briefcase on the table in the middle of the changing room.

'Today is our day,' he announced, trying to rally his troops.

He opened the briefcase and jaws all round the room dropped as he revealed £5,000 in used banknotes. No further words were required. This was as exceptional a bonus for the County players as they could have imagined.

The story goes that, with the score at 0–0 at half-time, Morris stood on the touchline at the beginning of the second half flashing the fingers on both his hands to signal to the players he was upping the bonus to £10,000.

The game finished all square at the end of 90 minutes. Newton, clearly desperate to be the chairman of a cup-winning side, raced to the line, clutching the briefcase in front of his face, rather like the Chancellor of the Exchequer on Budget day, and with raised hand once more flashed his fingers. The incentive had now reached £20,000. It did the trick and County lifted the cup.

Jim Hosie was a big favourite with Ross County fans in the seasons leading up to and beyond their first Highland League championship win in 1967.

They were interesting times at the club, as Frank Thomson's influence as chairman took hold and he lured professional players who hadn't hit if off with league clubs, or who were reaching their sell-by date, to Victoria Park. A job at his distillery and a house in Invergordon, ingredients that were clearly tempting to many in the 1960s and 1970s, were the carrots.

Hosie was just 23 years old when he accepted Thomson's offer, after the millionaire arrived in a gold-coloured Jaguar at his parents' tenement home in Hardgate, Aberdeen.

Hosie had just returned from a season playing with Barnsley in Division Three in England, before which he had spent four seasons with Aberdeen, where he had made only about 15 appearances.

'I returned home,' he recalled, 'and took a trip down to see Teddy Scott, the trainer at Pittodrie, and I mentioned I was keen to find a new club and one that might also give me a job.

'As luck would have it, Thomson turned up at Pittodrie the following day to ask Teddy if the Dons had any free transfers he could pick up. Teddy told him about me and the next thing he turned up at the home of my parents, his car causing the neighbours' curtains to twitch.

'I thought I'd give it a go for a year and return to Aberdeen. That was in 1963 and I'm still living in Invergordon, where I was given a house and a job.'

Hosie's time at Pittodrie saw him work under two managers, Davie Shaw, who signed him, and Tommy Pearson, who released him at the end of his fourth season there.

Those were the days of Freddie Martin, the Scotland goalkeeper, of the great wing-half Archie Glen, and of others like Jackie Hather, Bobby Wishart and Graham Leggat, who was on the point of leaving for Fulham when Hosie signed in 1958. Two years later, the Dons discovered Charlie Cooke.

This mesmerising footballer was sold on to Dundee four years later, and in 1966 he was transferred to Chelsea as a replacement for Terry Venables for a then record fee of £72,000, the equivalent of almost £1m in 2010. Scotland was fruitful ground for the big English clubs seeking fresh talent in those days.

'I played more or less every game for Barnsley,' Hosie said of his time at Oakwell, 'and I was surprised when the manager Johnny Steele freed me. You hear of managers being 20 years ahead of their time, he was 20 years behind the times.

'He played me on the wing and I had to stick there, despite me being an inside-forward. It was a good, competitive league, with teams like Coventry City, managed at that time by Jimmy Hill before he became a TV football pundit.'

Like many others, Jim Hosie was captivated by his chairman at Ross County, though surprised in those early days at the method used to pick the team.

'As I recall, there was no manager in place when I joined County. There was no money in football. When I signed I was on £6 a week and I had my wages from my day job.

'Alex Young, the former Aberdeen centre-half, had been at County for five years before me and just as I came in he had to give up because of an injury. Like many players, Alex was at Victoria Park after their better days had gone. That wasn't the case with me.'

Young, who died in March 2010, had indeed been the linchpin of the Aberdeen side of the 1950s and was part of their famous half-back line with Jackie Hather on his right and Archie Glen at left-half. He was part of the team that won the Scottish League championship for the first time in their history in 1954–55.

Three years later, he joined Ross County. He was 33 and appointed player-coach on a five-year contract, an agreement that enabled him to open a grocer's business in Fortrose, the only licensed grocer's and newsagents in the Black Isle at the time.

Alex Young.
(*Ross-shire Journal*)

These were barren years for County in terms of trophies, but Young, who led the club to a Scottish Cup second-round win over Dumbarton at Boghead in 1962, was rated the best defender in the Highland League.

As Young bowed out and Hosie arrived, the new boy was initially surprised by the method of selecting the starting line-up at Victoria Park.

'It was unusual,' he said. 'It was chosen by a committee of about a dozen men who used to meet on a Thursday night. You can imagine how that would have worked. Some wanted the players they selected in, and others argued for their nominees. I think it was about four o'clock in the morning sometimes before they agreed on the team.

'Sammy Wilson, who had been playing, took over as coach in my first year and Ian McNeill came in and we got a good team going which allowed us to start to threaten Inverness Caley and Elgin City.'

He laughed when remembering the Scottish Cup tie against Rangers in 1966. The cold and miserable weather on that Monday afternoon in February did not make for pleasant football or spectating. Yet, the ground was packed.

'Judging by the excuses people made to be at the game, there must have been about 5,000 funerals that day. The schools were empty, too, and there was an agreement from the head teachers to turn a blind eye. Maybe it was because the game had been postponed for two successive Saturdays and any kids would have had tickets.'

County had eliminated Forfar Athletic with a 4–3 win at home in preliminary round two of the Scottish Cup before rattling five goals past Alloa Athletic in an eight-goal thriller at Recreation Park in the first round proper.

Rangers went on to win the trophy that season, taking two games to defeat Celtic. The first, on 23 April 1966, drew a crowd of 126,552 to Hampden Park for a 0–0 draw while the replay, won by the only goal of the game, was watched by 98,202.

'There were several decent players in the County side at that time,' said Hosie, 'though in my opinion, Johnny MacKay, the left winger, a local boy, should and could have played for Scotland. However, he chose to go to Aberdeen University to study and was lost to the professional game. He was the most talented of our squad. 'In his own words, Don MacMillan is a 'Fitee loon' from Aberdeen who, like many other footballers whose potential, for one reason or another, was never fully fulfilled, found their niche in the Highland League.

Certainly, Ross County were delighted to secure his services in 1964, especially as he had been good enough seven years earlier to have been snapped up by Jimmy McGrory, the Celtic manager, and whisked off to Parkhead at a time when Charlie Tully, Bobby Evans, Neil Mochan and Bobby Collins wore the green and white hoops.

Jock Stein, cutting his coaching teeth with the reserves, took charge of Don and other youngsters like Stevie Chalmers, Bertie Auld, Mike Jackson and Alec Byrne, all keen to be given their chance for stardom.

No sooner had Don signed from Woodside juniors in Aberdeen than he found himself in the United States as part of a Celtic tour, during which he played two or three games. Willie Fernie was his room-mate during the trip and Don was excited to be among such illustrious company.

Fernie, a Fifer, was a renowned dribbler, often dubbed greedy because of his unwillingness to pass the ball to team-mates. Still, he had represented Scotland in two World Cup tournaments – in 1954 and 1958 – before MacMillan arrived at Parkhead. Like Sammy Wilson, Fernie had been part of the Celtic team that beat Rangers 7–1 in the 1957 League Cup final and, on his day, was a fabulously entertaining footballer.

But MacMillan found it hard to break into the first team, being kept out of the left-half position by the Northern Ireland international, Bertie Peacock. That, and a knee injury that McGrory concluded would end his career, saw him depart Parkhead after five years and he headed back to the Granite City and a season with Aberdeen.

'After a year at Pittodrie,' said Don, 'I signed for Elgin City in the Highland League, though I was out of there a year later as I didn't get on too well with one or two people and I thought the club messed me about by moving me from position to position when others were injured.

'Then, one day in 1964, Frank Thomson came down to see me in his Rolls Royce and signed me for Ross County. Sammy Wilson was the manager and they were trying to assemble a team to challenge for trophies.

'It was a very tough league to play in. There were a few choppers. Ally Chisholm, who played at Clachnacuddin, was a hard character. I used to nutmeg him and say, "You missed again, Ally" then knew he'd be after me for the remainder of the game.'

Don played with County until he was in his thirties, but returned later to help out Ian McNeill on the coaching side and unwittingly found himself in direct opposition to a player who was to become one of the biggest names in Scottish football.

'One day we went to play at Peterhead,' Don recalled, 'and Ian announced he had taken my boots with him. I was 40 years old and we must have been short of players because Ian ordered me to get stripped; I was to play at centre-half.

'I came up against a young centre-forward who was farmed out by Aberdeen. His name was Willie Miller, who went on to become a Dons legend and one of the game's best-ever defenders He didn't get a kick of the ball against me that day. That was my last game and I think we won 2–1.'

But, if Don had Frank Thomson to thank for his new life in the Highlands, it wasn't until the death of the former club chairman in Australia in December 1989 that he had the opportunity of repaying the man who gave him a distillery job as part of his deal in joining County. It was one final act that was to mark the former businessman's close links with his beloved Invergordon.

'His last wish was that his ashes should be scattered in the water at the foot of Distillery Brae. He had often argued with people who complained of debris coming from the distillery into the water and so, with his son, I took his ashes out in a boat and scattered them at the end of the outflow pipe. It was his way

of getting back at those who had complained.'

Willie Hamilton, one of football's many flawed geniuses, spent a largely unremarkable time at Victoria Park between 1969 and 1971, though nothing is recorded of his stay, save for the comment of a team-mate that he 'fell down drunk during one training session'.

Hamilton was in the twilight of a career that started in 1956 when, just 16 years old, he made his debut for Sheffield United, before going on to make 79 appearances in five years.

There followed employment at a string of clubs, but he rarely dallied for very long. A season at Middlesbrough was followed by another at Heart of Midlothian before Jock Stein, then manager of Hibernian and a great admirer of this talented forward, enticed him to Easter Road in 1963.

Two years later, Hamilton moved to Aston Villa, then returned to Hearts before finding his way north to Dingwall. He finished his career in the UK at Hamilton Accies in 1972, having gained one Scotland cap but, because of his lifestyle, never fulfilled the potential he had once displayed. Sojourns to Australia and South Africa fell flat and Willie Hamilton died of a heart attack in 1976.

Frank Thomson's flash cars often played their part in persuading players to join Ross County. And so it proved with a 16-year-old whizz-kid from Dornoch who, when he was 13 and still in short trousers, played for the under-14s, 15, 17s, the full men's team in Dornoch and the county men's team select.

The effervescent Calum Grant looked back with fondness to those times of energy and enthusiasm and a willingness to compete.

Tipped-off about the youngster who could score goals at any level, Thomson sought him out to offer him a trial with County and, when the moment arrived – an away game against Brora Rangers – the club chairman arrived in an open-top Mercedes to drive the youngster to the ground.

The young Calum was impressed – 'think of the psychology Thomson employed' – and a couple of days later he put pen to paper at Victoria Park.

Grant enjoyed four productive years with County despite, in his last season there, undertaking a heavy training and travelling scheduled as he worked and studied in Edinburgh for his travel and tourism qualifications.

'It was tiring,' he said. 'I trained with Hearts, travelled home on Friday night, played for County on the Saturday, either at home or places like Elgin, Peterhead or Buckie, travelled back to Dornoch after the game, then down to Edinburgh the following day. I became weary of it.'

He had already established himself as one of the 1967 heroes, those who lifted the first Highland League championship in County's history with a last-day win over Fraserburgh at Dingwall, and had admirers elsewhere.

'Sammy Wilson had moved on and Ian McNeill became the manager and I found it all a bit much for me,' he explained. 'Ian arranged with Gala Fairydean's manager Frank Duncan that I could go there on loan.

'I was in the same boat – training at Tynecastle and loaned to Gala – as my good friend Jim Jefferies, later to become the Hearts manager on two separate occasions with a lengthy stay at Kilmarnock in between. Jim and I travelled together, but the standard in the East of Scotland was not as high as it was in the Highland League and I started rattling in the goals. Before I knew where I was, I was invited to take part in a trial for Lincoln City in the Fourth Division in England.

'I played against Grimsby Town in the Lincolnshire Cup away from home at Blundell Park and scored after seven minutes. The adrenalin was pumping and I improved the longer the game went on, and then on the Saturday I scored a hat-trick for the reserves. I signed a contract on the Monday.'

Grant believes his sporting prowess came from his mother's side of the family, as his farmer father, Mac, had no interest in his son's past-times of football and golf. Calum was amused by this and found it endearing.

'My father would rather I had concentrated on my studies,' he said. But Grant senior did attend a big game at Dingwall in which his son was in action. 'I took part against Celtic at Victoria Park, a testimonial for Don MacMillan, and I arranged for my dad and a friend to have complimentary tickets.

'Afterwards, when he returned home to queries from my mother about how I had played, he said he thought I had done okay. And the score? He had no idea, but was full of information about meeting a farmer from the Black Isle and their conversation about some piece of agricultural equipment.'

At Lincoln, Calum teamed up with a clutch of other young lads keen to make their way in football; Graham Taylor, with whom he has retained a friendship, went on to become a top coach and manager of the England team, while Jim Smith, became known as a no-nonsense boss at leading clubs like Newcastle United, Birmingham City and Queen's Park Rangers.

Ray Harford was also in the team. He went on to manage several English Premier League clubs and was Kenny Dalglish's assistant when they won the championship with Blackburn Rovers in 1995.

There were many others in that Lincoln City side who went on to do well in the game, but bad fortune struck Grant after less than a year there when, during a game against Mansfield Town, he sustained what we now know as a cruciate ligament injury.

'The surgeon told me that my knee wouldn't be strong enough to play professional football again,' he said, 'but thought that after a period of rest I might be able to play part-time. In those days, knee problems were usually associated with cartilage injuries, but the surgeon identified it as a cruciate issue, unheard of at the time.

'Then one day I took a call at Lincoln City's ground from Frank Thomson, by then vice-president of Holiday Inns and based in Memphis, Tennessee. He'd heard of my injury and he offered me a job in America. It was ideal for me, given my tourism qualifications, and I saw out my contract at Lincoln in 1971 and headed west for another chapter in the travel business across the Atlantic.'

There was further misfortune, however, and before a year was out he was recalled home with the news that his mother had bowel cancer.

'My father told me we didn't know if she would survive six weeks or six years,' he recalled. 'But my mum was a fighter. She lived on for 29 more years.'

Calum was now home for good and took himself to Dingwall where,

ROSS COUNTY

From Highland League to Hampden

Calum Grant in his heyday as a County goal-scorer.

because he had his coaching badges from his time in England, he began to help Sandy Wallace, then in charge at County.

He was still in his early 20s and one match day, en route to a reserve game at Golspie, he was informed that one of the County players had taken ill on the bus. Hs services on the field of play were required.

'I scored a couple of goals,' he recalled, 'and six weeks later I was back in the first team.

'About 18 months or so after that, Sandy took over as manager of Clachnacuddin and Ian McNeill was back at County for his second spell. Sandy asked me to join him, but Ian refused to release me to Clach and told me he would only let me go if I went to Brora, where Sammy Wilson was now the manager. That was in 1974, and I played out the season before joining Clach, where we built the team that won the league and the Qualifying Cup. It was an incredible side.'

But Calum's link with County was re-established when he joined the board and took particular interest in youth development, a role over a period of ten years that he thoroughly enjoyed.

'Ross County are close to my heart,' he said, 'and I was lucky to have played for them in those great days of the 1960s.'

Derek Adams may have blotted out from his memory one of his early experiences as a young lad, fresh from failing in his efforts to establish a playing career with Burnley and eager to make an impact with his new club.

It was 1996 and Neale Cooper was the manager. The County squad were rewarded for their diligence with an end-of-season trip to Dublin with Johnston Bellshaw, Robbie Williamson and Billy Ferries tasked with picking up new boy Derek outside Perth.

'The arrangement was made that we would meet Derek at a lay-by near Perth,' Ferries remembered, 'at six o'clock in the morning then head for Glasgow for our flight to Ireland.

'Johnston, Robbie and I were brought up in the culture of the Highland League, which equated to treating football as a hobby and part of our social life. So, a trip away with the boys was going to be fun and games all the way.

'Robbie and I were in the back seat of Johnston's car and as we pulled into the lay-by to collect our passenger, Derek's dad George stepped forward to open the door for his son.

'He stooped to look into the vehicle to say hello, but quite what he thought when he saw me and Robbie in the back with a bottle of whisky in a car filled with the fumes of the cratur, I shudder to think. Whatever it was he masked it well, though for a teetotaller like George to hand his young lad into our care, so to speak, must have given him sleepless nights until Derek returned home safe and well a few days later.'

Bellshaw was a big, strapping centre-half from the Black Isle whose vision was far from 20/20. Ferries remembered an embarrassing incident when they played an uncompromising Fort William side at a misty, rain-swept Claggan Park.

'Johnston was having a shocker and was substituted. He didn't like it. He didn't have his contact lenses in and he stormed off in a furious huff and plumped himself down in the dugout full of rage and ranting that he hadn't deserved to be taken off. There were words of agreement from the dugout personnel and after a couple of minutes of complaining from the player with the wounded pride, somebody tapped him on the shoulder and said: "Johnston, you're in the wrong dugout." It was the Fort William lot who were egging him on telling him he was right to be angry.'

No-one who has ever been associated with Highland League football would need reminding of the game's inordinate number of characters. At County, there were servants like Davie Hamilton, who over decades at the club saw his duties range from kitman to masseur.

'I started going to support County when I was five years old,' Ferries said, 'and Davie was there to chase you away from areas you weren't meant to be in. He was a deaf mute and because he couldn't form words and would simply make a noise, we were terrified of him.'

Donnie MacBean reiterated the Ferries view that Hamilton was a club legend, the kind of constant required at organisations where managers and players come and go.

Davie Hamilton died in June 2005, aged 79. He had been associated with County for six decades, and at his funeral, MacBean paid a moving tribute to the man known as Mr Ross County.

'At the early age of four-and-a-half,' said Donnie, 'Davie was sent to Donaldson's School in Edinburgh for the deaf and dumb, staying there until he was 16 when he returned to Dingwall to start his apprenticeship as a cobbler, a trade he worked at until his retirement.

'A few seasons back when the team were playing in Edinburgh, as we passed the school, the excitement on Davie's face as there for all to see, showing how much he had enjoyed his time there.

'On his return home, he turned to football in his spare time, as a committee man with the Queens of the North, and refereeing, a role at which he commanded the greatest respect on the field. When anyone tried to take advantage of his handicap and used bad language, he simply lip-read and then took the necessary action.'

Davie Hamilton filled many positions at Ross County, apart from manager, although it was pointed out that this did not prevent him from offering his opinion to all who took on that job.

'He travelled the length and breadth of Scotland on the team bus as co-pilot to our driver, Tony Fraser,' said Donnie. 'He was known and welcomed in all opposition boardrooms, judging them by the brand of whisky they served; a Famous Grouse was his favourite tipple.

'Davie reached Victoria Park on his bike early every morning, always finding something that needed his attention. To say he was a Ross County legend would be an understatement.'

There were others, too, who played their part in keeping the club ticking over, as Billy Ferries proclaimed.

'Davie and Chic Ogilvie, another fantastic character and a great servant to Ross County in a number of roles, were the real foundations of the club and their contribution was enormous.

'Chic, who died in 2005, was kitman when Neale Cooper was there, but over the years he had played for County and had a spell as manager.

'He was also a kind of mentor to some of the players, and I remember one day before a game I was in his little room and mentioned I was feeling a bit under the weather. He ordered me to sit down and poured me a large glass of Whyte & Mackay.

'I played well in the first half, then in the interval, I went back to Chic's room for another dram for the second half. Goodness knows what Neale would have thought had he known.

'I kept out of his way in the dressing room in case he smelled the fumes. But Chic was a man you couldn't refuse.'

There were others who Ferries considered cornerstones of Ross County, unsung heroes who were important to the club.

'George Barnetson, the groundsman, did so much for County. So, too, in his way, did Willie Wilson, who covered the team for the local newspaper. Sometimes he would slag us off but at the same time you knew he was on your side.'

There were others who played their part in the history of County. Irene Ross, later to marry chairman Robert Shearer, was at Victoria Park as secretary for 30 years. There were many who gave years of unstinting service and who were all so important to County.

Ferries had more than one spell with the Staggies, a club he served with distinction and with which he was rated highly, as he straddled their time in the Highland League and the SFL.

The right winger from the village of Edderton, near Tain, was just 16 when he joined County under Robbie Giles, the manager at the time. Giles had been a well-known defender with Clachnacuddin in his playing days.

By the time Ferries made his first-team debut, against Elgin City at Borough Briggs, and within a dozen games of season 1983–84 starting, Donald Stewart had taken charge.

Billy Ferries played for the Staggies for four years before deciding, at the age of 20, to take the unusual step for one so young and start his own business.

'I worked as a kitchen fitter,' he said, 'and got things underway with a loan through the government's youth opportunity scheme. In order to build up the business I decided to stop playing for a couple of years. Instead, I played in the North reserve league, but turned out for a few games for County in midweek matches.

'Then, in 1987 I returned to Victoria Park under Bobby Wilson, a manager you really wanted to play for, someone who could motivate you.

'He allowed you freedom on the park and was ahead of previous managers. I left in 1990 and joined Elgin City under Steve "Pelé" Paterson for a year. I needed some extra money at the time and County didn't offer me much by way of a signing-on fee.

'I think the offer was £700 and I wanted £1,000. There was a deadlock and I left. A year later I returned when they said, "You can have whatever you want," and I told them I'd have the £1,000 they never gave me the previous time.'

Ferries had won the treble with Elgin, then the Highland League title with County in 1991 and again the following year. He stayed on when they entered the Third Division and remained until the title was won under Cooper.

'The club changed when Neale came in,' he said. 'They started to go down the route of having full-time players and the transition was quite difficult for the part-time players.

'When Bobby was manager, it was very much a team of local lads and guys like Willie Furphy and Billy Herd were brought in and did well for the club.'

Herd had 131 appearances while Furphy, a London-born defender, was five years at County and amassed 105 appearances. He'd come from Elgin City but had started off his career with Ayr United, then Kilmarnock, Montrose and Dumbarton. Both he and Herd were lured north for £4 a week, according to Ferries.

'Neale did very well. There were a lot of players coming in and out and he got promotion in his third season.

'But we had players like John Hewitt, the former Aberdeen winger, Danny Crainie, the much-travelled ex-Celtic, who played just five games for us, goalkeeper Nicky Walker, who'd been at Motherwell and Aberdeen, and Alec Taylor, another ex-Motherwell player. There were so many came up. Some stayed around, others left soon after arriving.'

By his own admission, Ferries had 'gone a little bit stale' under Wilson and

Billy Ferries (right) and Ivan Golac, who managed Dundee United in their only other Scottish Cup win – in 1994 – parade the Scottish Cup before the big game kicked-off. (*Material Marketing & Communications*)

Neale Cooper and his squad celebrate winning the Division Three championship in 1999. (*Ken Macpherson*)

went through the motions rather than putting in the effort required now that the club was established in the SFL.

'Neale basically told me I'd have to get my finger out if I wanted to remain in the team and that gave me a little jolt and pushed me on. I was 30 or 31 and needed that kick up the backside.

'We sensed there was a greater ambition at the club, with more and more full-time players being taken on. By the time I left, nearly all the players were full-time. I finished when we won the Third Division title in 1999.

'I was told I could have stayed another year, but I was virtually the only part-time player left and the club had outgrown me. I joined Brora Rangers and managed them a few years later as well.'

Alistair MacDonald captained Ross County in the 1930s. He was unable to attend the Scottish Cup final against Dundee United, but the 94-year-old tuned-in to hear the game on the radio in his Evanton home.

A former forestry worker on the Novar Estate, near his home, MacDonald was full of praise for the Staggies of today, but cast his mind back to when he joined County in 1934 after playing for local teams, Black Rock Rovers and Alness United. He may have had a two-year spell with Clachnacuddin after the outbreak of the Second World War, but Alistair was a County man through and through.

During the war he was attached to the bomb disposal unit and was based in Sussex and Kent. He rejoined County after the war ended and stayed at Victoria Park until 1950, meaning his service with the club of which he was made captain in 1938, when he was only 23, was extremely long.

Opposite.
Alistair MacDonald, 94 and still supporting the team he played for in the 1930s. (*dgordonphotography.co.uk*)

But MacDonald, a lifelong Hibernian supporter, was delighted to be at the Scottish Cup quarter-final reply between the Edinburgh side and County at

54

Victoria Park with his granddaughter Cherie Pumphrey alongside him acting as match commentator because of his failing sight.

He could still recite the famous five forward line of the 1950s – Smith, Johnstone, Reilly, Turnbull and Ormond – which he used to watch, and experienced mixed loyalties on the night, but he was delighted County reached the cup final after beating Celtic on the way.

'I don't see any reason why they can't get promoted,' he said. 'They have a fine team and a talented manager.'

Barry Wilson knows all about the Chinese whispers inside and outside football over allegations of nepotism.

Derek Adams went through much of his career carrying accusations that he was only in the game because of the influence of his father George, County's director of football.

Wilson played under his father Bobby for Ross County as he led them to two Highland League crowns and into the Scottish Football League's Third Division, but was subjected to slurs from some members of his own team, who resented him, and from a section of the Victoria Park support, whose comments were along the lines of 'you only get a game because you father's the manager'.

'In some ways, that toughened me up for the rest of my career,' said Barry. 'It was awkward at the start and in that first season I was used mainly as a substitute.'

Wilson was doing so well in the Highland League that the former Clach manager Roshie Fraser tipped-off someone he knew at Southampton that they should have a look at the County winger.

'They watched me a couple of times and the deal was done with Ian Branfoot, the Southampton manager, who agreed to pay County £25,000 for the transfer. It was 1992, the first year of the Premiership in England and I was just 20 years old. It was a big experience, but the club put me into digs with a family with two daughters and there were no boys to bond with. I just couldn't settle, despite training alongside some great players like Alan Shearer and Matthew Le Tissier.'

His time on the south coast was to last barely three months as it became clear he was unhappy, and while he now looks back with 'what might have been' thoughts, he has every reason to be proud of a playing career that saw him perform at the top level in Scottish football.

Branfoot's arm-twisting for him to remain at Southampton proved fruitless and Wilson returned to County with the transfer fee having to be repaid, albeit it in instalments starting with a £10,000 deposit because Wilson senior had spent the money on new recruits.

'In 1994, County's first season in the SFL, we met Raith Rovers in the League Cup. Jimmy Nicholl, the Starks Park manager, saw something in me and made a quick move to take me to the Fife club, then in the First Division, and one my dad used to manage. The fee was £40,000.

'Raith hadn't enjoyed a good start to their campaign and had clearly under-achieved. Then, soon after I arrived, they picked up and went on a great run and we won the league title on the last day of the season and promotion to the Premier League.

'They also went on to win the League Cup with an astonishing 6–5 penalties win over Celtic in the final after a 2–2 draw, but the downside was that I was cup-tied because of the earlier game between them and Ross County.'

Nicholl's departure for Millwall brought in a new manager, Jimmy Thomson, promoted from his role in charge of the youth team.

'We didn't hit it off,' Wilson said, 'and I turned down the derisory offer they made me to stay on. They freed me in the summer 1996, news that came as a shock given that it was contained in a letter which was waiting for me when I arrived home from my honeymoon.

'I had spoken to my dad about going back to County but lo and behold he was sacked and I felt I couldn't return to Victoria Park. It would have been unworkable.

'Had he not been sacked, I would probably have ended up there rather than at their great rivals, Inverness Caledonian Thistle, which is where I went for training facilities, and Steve Paterson, the manager, asked me to sign. They were in the Third Division, but we won the league title in that season, my first with the club.

Wilson was five seasons at Caley. Then in 2000, Livingston, where Jim Leishman and Davie Hay were in charge, came in with a bid of close on £100,000.

The West Lothian club were in the First Division and Caley Thistle had also won promotion to that league. Then, Wilson's new employers stormed to promotion and he found himself once more a Premier League player.

'I had a very good time at Livingston and probably played some of the best football of my career there. I scored 16 goals from midfield in that promotion-winning season and 12 in the Premier League, the club's top scorer.

'We finished third that season, a remarkable achievement, and I profited from playing alongside people like David Fernandez and Stuart Lovell.

'The following season we finished sixth or seventh and they brought in a Brazilian coach, Marcio Maximo. After one training session I knew it wasn't for me. I was wary of his ability to coach and I spoke to Leishman about it, but it was too late.'

John Robertson, then in charge at Caley Thistle, knew Wilson was unhappy and he jumped at the chance to return to the Caledonian Stadium. Ironically Maximo, British football's first Brazilian boss, was sacked soon after. He lasted just nine games – three wins, three defeats and three draws – but Livingston picked themselves up and went on to win the League Cup that year under Davie Hay and Wilson began to think: 'What if …?'

'But I was delighted to be back at Inverness,' he said, 'and I helped them to graduate to the Premier League in my first season. Winning promotions in my first seasons with teams was a bit of a trend and I was proud to be on the scoresheet on the last day of the season when we beat St Johnstone 3–1. Paul Ritchie and David Bingham got the other goals and we went up to the top division.'

Barry Wilson looked back with fondness on his beginnings at Ross County and spoke of his admiration for Derek Adams and the exciting young team he assembled, which powered their way to Hampden on 15 May 2010.

It's all changed at Victoria Park since those days of the Highland League and the early years in the Third Division.

'In the Highland League, you were paid £4 a week,' he remembered, 'and they took £1 off you for the club draw, which was compulsory. You got a tenner if you won, which was spent on drink on the way back from a game. It was all about enjoyment.

'There was one time in those crazy days that I played for County against Caley in the Highland League at Telford Street. For some reason I had a T-shirt under my strip which belonged to Gordon Connelly. He'd had it made up for a previous occasion and when I scored a goal directly from a corner kick, I ran down the length of the park to the County fans, and lifted my jersey to expose the message: Let's laugh at Caley.

'Gordon had it printed when we won our league title in 1991 and I wore it that day. There was no malice. Just a laugh, but a local newspaper blew it up and I was embarrassed and apologetic. Thank goodness the Caley fans forgave me.

'As for Derek Adams, wel, he has proved, as I did, that having a father in the game and at the same club can have its drawbacks, but that it was our talents that got us through and gave us success.'

Gordon MacRae, the County vice-chairman, is standing by for the time when his beloved team is ready to enter the Scottish Premier League.

Plans for a major revamp of Victoria Park have already been passed for such an eventuality and, because of his background in the construction industry – his company was among the leading house-builders in the North and North-east – his brief will be to bring about the necessary changes at the ground.

He carried out a similar exercise before a County progressed through the leagues to the First Division. There was a major refurbishment, a new east stand, a restructure of the Jail End enclosure and the installation of new turnstiles and floodlighting.

'I have no doubt we're headed for the SPL,' MacRae said, 'and when we win promotion, I'll be ready to go into action.'

Gordon MacRae's links with County go back to his teen years, when he graduated from the feeder team, Queens of the North, to play for the Highland League club.

'Those were different, less professional days,' he said. 'Frank Thomson was the main man and at one point he even chose the team.

'I remember him giving me a lift in his car from Inverness to my home in Beauly after I finished work. We had a Highland League Cup game against Inverness Thistle in Dingwall that night and on the drive home he asked me to play centre-forward.

'He dismissed my protest that, as I was not a centre-forward – I played inside-right – and I didn't think it would be a good idea. So after I'd had my tea, I jumped in a Bedford van with a pal of mine and headed off for Victoria Park.

'The crowds were so big and traffic going nowhere that I got out of the van, told my friend to park it and raced off for the ground, fearing I would be too late to play.

'When I reached the changing room, Davie Hamilton, who did every imaginable job at County, pushed me into a chair, yanked off my clothes and threw a strip at me. Because he was a deaf mute, all he could do was make noises, although it was clear he was not happy about my lack of punctuality.

'He pointed toward the pitch, urging me to get out there and I had a warm-up of about two minutes before the match kicked-off.'

Gordon Connelly is never happier than when around football and footballers. That is why he clung on to a playing career that took him to several Highland League clubs and which ended only in the spring of 2009, at the age of 42.

But because 'Ross County is my club' and he was desperate to regain his connection with Victoria Park, the former midfielder was keen to return to the fold.

He had finished his career at Brora Rangers and contacted Derek Adams, a team-mate from the Neale Cooper era, and offered his services as a coach. He was invited on board to help with the players' pre-match warm-ups, and a year after battling with Brora in the basement of the Highland League he was in the dugout at Hampden.

'I learned more from Derek and Craig Brewster in one season than I ever did in all my years in the game,' he said. 'It's clear that Derek is destined for big things.

'I am so happy to be involved and what a season it was; two fantastic Scottish Cup quarter-final ties against Hibs and two appearances at Hampden, all wonderful occasions. It certainly softened the blow of not playing anymore. Derek put together a fantastic side that played superb football all season. I just wish I was younger. I would have loved to have played in his team.'

Connelly's stay in the Highlands was supposed to be temporary. As Bobby Wilson moved into the manager's chair in 1987, he saw the young lad from Stirling, whom he had coached at Dunfermline, as someone around whom he could structure his side around to challenge for the Highland League title.

The Pars had just won promotion to the Premier League and Jim Leishman, their manager, needed more experience in his team to consolidate the East End Park side's status in the top flight.

'I knew it was going to be tough for me to break in to Leishman's plans,' he said. 'I had been there three-and-a-half years and was a first-team regular, winning promotions from the Second and First Divisions, but it became clear I would be out in the cold and I wanted to play.'

Lodging with his new boss and his wife Jessie, and sharing a room with their son Barry, Connelly, who hadn't heard of Ross County nor knew where Dingwall was prior to his first visit, arrived as a temporary employee. He 'forgot to go home'.

'I arrived and saw this wee cowshed of a building on the side of the pitch,' he said. 'But I loved the club and the area and felt right at home.

'The Highland League was a good league at the time with excellent clubs like Inverness Caledonian, Inverness Thistle, Elgin City and Peterhead. It was strong and I saw it potentially as a way of stepping back up a level.'

He didn't know quite what to expect at first but admitted that, during the warm-up for his County debut, the team's elder statesman surprised him.

'I was paired with Don Cowie senior as we prepared before the game, and he quickly made me realise when I saw him pinging the ball about that I had arrived at a half-decent team. Most of the players were local but Bobby had done well at Keith and therefore had a good idea of the players who were around.

'There was Donald MacKay and James McKay, probably two of the most talented players I came across in the Highlands. Donald was a left-sided player and had many of Britain's top clubs chasing him at one point, but he refused to leave the area. James, a striker, had been at Hibs when he was younger.'

Connelly had come through the ranks at Dunfermline with Norrie McCathie, John Watson and Ian McCall. His decision to remain at Dingwall, however, was not a difficult one.

'I could see that there was the making of something at County. The Highland League was vibrant and we used to get crowds of 5,000 at Victoria Park when we played the likes of Caley and Elgin and others. It was a very competitive league with a good standard.'

It was a happy time for Gordon Connelly, made all the more enjoyable when County won entry to the Third Division and his family, based in Stirling, could see him in action at places like Alloa, East Stirling and Cowdenbeath.

The ecstasy was followed by the agony of the departure in 1996 of Bobby Wilson, the man who had taken him north and, by his own admission, things were never the same again.

'It was a massive blow to me when Bobby was sacked,' he said. 'He was a father figure to me and life changed, especially when Neale Cooper came in and decided to impose changes which, at first, didn't include me.

'He had a view that those who were there under Bobby weren't good enough. He wanted his own players in and it was tough for me because I was seen as County's big player, the one Bobby had built his team around.

'Neale wanted to show he could do the job without me. So, for the first seven games he didn't play any of Bobby's players and he lost all of those matches. But he bowed to pressure and reinstated those he'd dropped and we went on a great run and finished third in the league.'

Those early weeks under the new regime were fraught and difficult. Connelly felt unfairly treated with double training sessions ordered for him, or attempts to marginalise him during sessions.

'Cooper tried to break me,' he claimed, 'hoping I would leave. I wasn't prepared to do that. Ross County was my club.

'The manager respected that I worked hard, and when I went back into the team I became his skipper, but there was such an influx of players – he used

Opposite.
Gordon Connelly.
(Ken Macpherson)

more than 70 in one season – that it sometimes created disharmony.

'Those at the club when the new manager arrived were on £5 a week and players like John Hewitt, a Gothenburg hero with Cooper in Aberdeen's glory years but by then way past his best, were receiving hundreds of pounds a week. I couldn't handle that. So, something had to give and, as no player is bigger than the club, it was agreed I would leave.'

County and Connelly parted company in March 1997, his decade at Dingwall marked by a testimonial game against Heart of Midlothian.

'I fielded a select team of all the old players,' he added, 'and made Bobby the manager. That didn't go down too well but it was my night and the decision was mine.'

Connelly's subsequent travels took him to Wick Academy, followed by Forres Mechanics where, after three years at the heart of their midfield, he became player-assistant manager under Dave Milroy, an ex-Caley man, and then Fraser Kellas.

'When Fraser moved on I was appointed player-manager and I thoroughly enjoyed it. It was probably the most memorable time I had in football because I won two Highland League Cups in a row and took them to the third round of the Scottish Cup, going out to Dundee United at Tannadice, after we had beaten East Stirling in an earlier round.'

Connelly was forced out of football for a year-and-a-half after being struck down with a life-threatening illness, a rare condition that saw an abscess grow on his spinal chord at the back of his neck.

He had to rebuild his confidence and he made a comeback with Brora Rangers for a few games before being appointed Steve Paterson's playing assistant at Forres.

'Steve was the daddy of them all in terms of winning championships and trophies in the Highland League,' he proclaimed. 'He had the Midas touch with players, too; they all wanted to play for him.'

Still a fit and industrious midfielder, Connelly took the road to Clachnacuddin for a time before bringing his playing career to a close at Brora.

He has fond memories of his days in the middle of the Ross County team, however, and the many talented team-mates he worked with at that time.

So, was there one who stood out? 'The best player in my ten years at County was Chris Somerville. He was a fantastic right-back, but just a couple of inches too short for bigger clubs to take a risk with.

'I loved my time under Bobby Wilson and in some ways I regret having to move as County was my club, but I couldn't watch someone destroy it. Maybe had I been a bit more mature I might have hung on, but in the end he [Neale Cooper] would have still kept bringing in players and I wouldn't have been given a game.'

Who could have predicted that 14 years after he severed connections with County, Connelly would be back with them and part of the biggest day in their history?

THE ADAMS ETHOS
INFLUENCES THE STAGGIES

Football's bush telegraph went into overdrive when Derek Adams left Burnley in 1996 after a disappointing period. What next for the promising midfield player?

Dad George, highly respected as a youth coach in Scotland, was employed by Celtic at the time, scouting for and developing young talent. He felt his son, just 21 years old, might benefit from a step down from the cut and thrust of English football and he spoke with Neale Cooper, manager at Ross County at the time.

It was a telephone call that would lead to an enduring association with County and its principal benefactor, Roy MacGregor, then the club chairman.

Derek did well at County as a player. In two seasons, he scored more than

Star-maker George Adams.
(*Ken Macpherson*)

50 goals before being transferred to Motherwell for £200,000, with the chairman helping facilitate the personal terms between his departing player and his new employers.

'Roy negotiated good terms for Derek,' George explained. 'He and I always kept up, and when I was at Rangers in charge of youth development, I loaned Graeme Smith, the goalkeeper, and Charlie Adam, the midfielder, to County as part of their football development.

'I did that because I knew the structure of the club and that they would be looked after in Dingwall. I built up a relationship with Roy and he had always said that he hoped at some stage we would work together. Later, when I left Rangers, he was in touch almost immediately to see if I might join County.'

George Adams's 45 years in football, working as Alex Ferguson's man in charge of youth in the halcyon days of Aberdeen, then at Celtic under Tommy Burns and Martin O'Neill, highlighted his worth to football clubs as he unearthed the kind of young players who could evolve into the stars of tomorrow.

Fir Park was to be his next port of call after leaving Parkhead, by which time his son was already established in the Motherwell first team. In time, George transferred his talents to the Lanarkshire club, where he brought through a clutch of bright young stars, like James McFadden, David Clarkson and Steven Hammell.

His Christian ethos is important, too, in how he conducts his business. Born in Glasgow, he attended Queen's Park School, and while there tragedy struck when his father died. George was just 11 years old and his mother, a cleaner who would leave home at 4.30am to clean the offices of the Prudential insurance company, raised him, his two sisters and his brother in difficult times.

'My mother would be back in the house to give us breakfast, pack us off to school, then head back out to clean somewhere else before returning for lunch,' he said.

His memory bank has many such childhood deposits.

'We are a very close family because of how we were brought up,' he said, 'and the work ethic my mother promoted was an example to my sisters, brother and me. It carried us through our lives and we're thankful for it.'

Football was the passport to a new life for a young George, who joined Aberdeen as a player in 1968 but, troubled by a knee injury that required eight operations, his time at Pittodrie reached a conclusion just three years later.

Doctors told him his career was over, but he returned to Glasgow and, despite going under the surgeon's knife on two more occasions, he went on to play for Partick Thistle, Clyde and East Stirlingshire before gravitating towards the Highland League, where he joined Buckie Thistle for a couple of seasons.

With his knee problem by then rendering it impossible for him to continue playing, Adams took on the role of manager at Fraserburgh and lifted them from the bottom of the league to runners-up in his two years there.

That success was followed by eight-and-a-half years as youth coach at Aberdeen, after which he took charge of Keith, then Peterhead. It was to be an apprenticeship in coaching that was to stand him in good stead.

After his impressive and highly recognised work at Motherwell, Rangers came calling. Would he take over the running of their youth set-up at Murray Park?

The Adams conveyor belt of aspiring young talent was at full throttle until a clash of personalities between him and Martin Bain, the Ibrox chief executive, intervened, prompting an inevitable parting of the ways.

Invited to elaborate on the issue and reveal any potential juicy gossip, Adams merely smiles. 'We fell out. Things didn't work out with him and me.' If there is anger and animosity within the Adams heart and mind, it will never be given a public airing. Whatever the reasons for their clashes – and the phrase 'chalk and cheese' comes to mind when comparing their respective styles – it resulted in the Rangers youth development chief walking away, in December 2005, from a job he loved. He was able to boast that, during his tenure with the club, he turned out 17 youth internationals, among them John Fleck and Danny Wilson.

To many outside football, George Adams might seem to be out of place in a sport known for its Machiavellian methods. Christian and principled, he has never striven for fame or glory. Yet, how, in almost half a century at his chosen trade, has he coped with the more industrial nature of the game?

'Ah, the swearing question,' he laughed. 'I don't swear, but I don't have a problem with it. On the other hand, people respect it and tend not to use bad language in my company.

'If you look at our football club, the discipline comes from the manager. If you have high standards in life, you try to pass them on. It's basics, like the please and thank you that parents taught their children. You need to breed that in a football club.

'There are players in all parts of the country and from all walks of life who haven't been fortunate enough to have been brought up like that.

'I remember a player came into the ground one day with a hat on and we told him that wasn't the done thing. Wee things like that are important.

'You don't hear bad language around the place. Why? Because it's not the done thing, although I think it's partly out of respect for me and for Derek.

'The teamwork and camaraderie at the club in the past couple of years have made things very enjoyable. I haven't witnessed many better dressing rooms, and I've been in the game for 45 years.

'I had a player, no longer at the club but who was in the team that won promotion to the First Division, whose mother came to me and told me she was now having conversations with her son without him swearing. I could have cried. That told me that parents see the development of their own son. How important is that?

'We're here to try and improve young men as football players. But, through the holistic approach, if we can play a part in helping develop them and to make them better persons, then I think we have a duty to do that.'

The Adams family sing from the same hymn sheet on this topic, although George declares a need for more money should County wish to step up and play with the big boys.

ROSS COUNTY

From Highland League to Hampden

'There needs to be realism of where the club wants to go. We need to look at the budgets and what it is possible to achieve.

'I accept that any club that isn't community based – that the community doesn't form part of the football club – isn't being run properly. After all, the basis of your club should be within your community. That's what Roy MacGregor wants.

'We are seen as the nicest football club in Scotland. You can still be that and still want to be somewhere else.

'There's a soft mentality and that's what I'd want to change. If you look at our operation, it could be argued that we have emphasised the youth side more than the first team.

'Recruitment, coaching and facilities are the important components in football. Ten, 20 and 30 years ago, we didn't have the facilities in Scotland, but we still had good players.

'The facilities are number three on the list. The coaching, of course, is important, but as in cooking, for example, if you don't have the proper ingredients, you're not going to be able to produce a good meal.

'When I started as a scout, the first thing you discuss is: Can a young player pass the ball? Can he control the ball?

'Nowadays, the first thing they ask is: Is he six foot two? Can he run like the wind? Is he strong?

'So, what we're now looking at is a different kind of player from what we had in the past. If you look at the Spaniards, I don't see Iniesta, Xavi, Messi being six foot two and running like the wind. They can all control a ball and pass it. They have great movement and great technique. We don't practise enough in this country, and no matter where you are or what you do, if you don't practise you won't get anywhere. We pay lip service to it in Scotland; I don't care what anybody says.'

Adams scoffed at the so-called distractions placed before today's youngsters; computers and other technology, constant TV, computer games and the like. He pointed to other countries producing top quality players as Scotland continues to lag behind.

'People talk about the distractions that stop kids playing football and improving their game. Are those distractions not around in Holland and France and Germany and other parts of the world?

'I did my youth director's award in Belgrade with Partisan and Red Star in 2006. Serbia was a war-torn country yet the kids are there at seven o'clock in the morning being coached. Can you imagine me suggesting that to parents? They would go off their heads.

'When I went to Celtic as youth coach, the youngsters were in two nights a week. I increased it to three. It was the same when I joined Rangers. It wasn't enough.

'When people of my generation were young, we would play football as soon as we got home from school every night. That doesn't happen any more.

'Our standards in Scotland have dropped. We are world champions at excuses and world champion talkers. Let's get back to reality.

ROSS COUNTY

From Highland League to Hampden

Opposite.
Scott Morrison, the ex-Aberdeen and Dunfermline full-back, expresses his joy after his Staggies team-mate Martin Scott scored a late second goal against Celtic.
(*Press & Journal*)

'Kids used to be comfortable with the ball. If they're not comfortable with the ball they're not going to play at a higher level. We need to get that back and stop trying to cover up for our own inadequacies.'

In the wake of their remarkable Scottish Cup run in 2009–2010, Adams pleaded for realism from within Ross County FC, a club punching well above its weight but working on a shoestring. First Division rivals like Dundee and Dunfermline, clubs with long histories, had found it extremely difficult to win their way into the SPL, despite each having considerably higher budgets than that on the table at Victoria Park.

He was proud that, under his son, the team had held its own in a hugely competitive league, as Derek had managed to squeeze the best from his dedicated players. There was, he opined, more to come from that team.

He surveyed the County squad in that glorious season which ended with the Scottish Cup final and expressed joy that it contained players who had been rejected by other, bigger clubs yet had moved to County and invited the management team to pull something extra from them. Their determination to haul themselves back up to where they felt they belonged was admirable.

'Too often in this country, we write off young players too soon; we don't like them they've got a spotty face, they talk back, we can't handle them. We're not prepared to sit down and talk to them and discuss problems. It's a man-management issue and we don't spend enough time on it.

'At County, there are players like Michael Gardyne, who played nine games for the team in 2008–09. Four of our team were in the running for the 2010 First Division player of the year and he was one of them.

'Scott Morrison couldn't get a game at County for a while. Yet, he wasn't out of the team in 2009–10 and did exceptionally well. That wasn't just down to the players. It's down to the way they've been treated, the way the team played and getting better performances out of every player.'

The training facilities at Victoria Park are the envy of many clubs in the Premier League, let alone the lower divisions. The indoor area boasts three full-size grass parks and a training area, as well as an old-style astro-turf pitch.

It is a set-up, George Adams insisted, that would not have been constructed had Roy MacGregor not been at Ross County. 'Roy's foresight has been crucial,' he added.

For all that football is a vital part of the life of George Adams, however, it is his family that takes pride of place; wife Moira and daughter Leigh-anne, who have never missed a Ross County game since Derek re-joined them in 2006, even if they have to drive from the family home in Lanarkshire at all hours of the day and night to support the Staggies.

'In any walk of life, you need the support of your family, and not a tenuous support either. We are so fortunate because there are people who don't enjoy that kind of backing.

'People involved with me in youth football used to criticise parents, labelling them a pain in the neck. They're not. I love seeing a dad or a mum taking their son to training, but we have a parents' charter and a players' charter with guidelines so everyone knows the parameters.

'We ask the parents to accept that striving to win is more important than winning itself; to avoid pressurising children about winning or losing; to be a role model for their child in relation to sporting behaviour; to show the benefits of teamwork, health and exercise; to help their children focus on the process of participation rather than the outcome. In other words, when your wee boy comes home after a game, ask how he played, not what the score was.

'The boys are instructed to show good sportsmanship and respect to others; to display sporting behaviour; to respect the rules and take pride in doing their best. We tell them to turn up promptly; make sure their boots are always clean; set their own standards and take pride in their appearance.

'We want them to make an effort to eat the right foods, take the pre- and post-match warm-up seriously and remember that, as they are representing Ross County Football Club, their behaviour on and off the park must be of the highest standard.

'We do report cards so parents know how their child is progressing, and if you do that, then everyone knows what's happening.'

The downside to dealing with children with stars in their eyes – telling them at some stage that they will not make the grade – is as tough for George Adams today as it was when he first he entered youth coaching.

'The saddest thing is taking a boy aside, a kid who has been at a club for three or four years and, maybe by the time he is 16, having to tell him we're not taking him to the next stage.

'When that happens, it's important that you have an entry policy and an exit policy. When you bring in a youngster, because you want him, the red carpet, so to speak, is rolled out. When you are releasing them, it's important to treat them the same way. If you don't have a proper strategy, it should not come as a shock.'

It is the people at Ross County, the fabric of the club, who command the greatest respect from this man who knows his way round football and has worked under a long list of members of the close-knit managerial fraternity, from Sir Alex Ferguson and Kenny Dalglish to Terry Butcher and Eric Black.

'People like Donnie MacBean, the club secretary who's been at the club for 46 years, had a tear in his eye when we beat Celtic. I had a tear in my eye as well. I was talking to people immediately afterwards and sometimes I just had to walk away because I became too emotional.

'I was so proud of the players, so proud of my son; the way they handled it. And I was so pleased for Roy MacGregor, Dave Siegel, our chairman, and the other directors and everyone connected with the club.

'When you see the amount of time and effort and finance they have put into Ross County over a long period, it's pleasing that they were rewarded by being part of a club that has appeared in a Scottish Cup final. It was their day in the sun.'

ROSS COUNTY
_____

From Highland League
to Hampden

DINGWALL: A GREAT PLACE
TO START THE COUNTY'S KIDS

George Adams knows all about the need to surround himself with capable lieutenants. It was important, therefore, to install the right man to head Ross County's youth system from which it is hoped a stream of youngsters will be developed for the first-team.

Davie Kirkwood, was a youth coach at Rangers' Murray Park academy before being lured north by Adams.

The former East Fife, Rangers, Heart of Midlothian, Airdrie and Raith Rovers player did, however, recognise that while County's youth set-up had a reputation as one of the best in the business, the remoteness of the club meant that the youngsters he oversaw would have to be doubly dedicated.

There are youth players from as far away as the Isle of Skye and Mallaig who have a two-and-a-half-hour drive simply to meet the team coach in Inverness for away games. Then there are two-and-a-half hours on the bus before they arrive for fixtures in Edinburgh or Glasgow.

There is no way round this issue, as Kirkwood explained how youth development is the way forward for County, partly because of the difficulties in encouraging established professionals to relocate to the Highlands.

'If players from the central belt want to move to England, which is six or seven hours away,' he said, 'what's the harm in coming two-and-a-half hours up the A9? There's no problem going to Aberdeen, which is the same distance away.

'I don't think travelling is a factor. We make the trip every week with two youth teams to Glasgow, yet they have a problem coming up to us once a year from the central belt. They moan about the distance, but we have kids from as far away as Skye, Elgin, Thurso, and they have enormous distances to travel. We do it because it's important for our kids to compete at that level.'

County's success in reaching the final of the Scottish Cup, and the profile it gave the club, could be a powerful selling point in their bid to attract good quality youngsters and for them to believe they might have a better chance of developing at Dingwall than at one of the big clubs. But there's a rider: 'If a kid only has aspirations of playing for Ross County,' Kirkwood added, 'he shouldn't play football. If they want to become a professional player, they must be looking to play at the highest level possible. If you want to earn loads of money, it's not going to be in Scotland.

'The bread and butter of Scottish football needs to be youth, because we don't have the finance to go and get a Brian Laudrup or a Paul Gascoigne any more. In youth development, the first thing you need isn't facilities or coaches, it's the players.

ROSS COUNTY

*From Highland League
to Hampden*

Ross County's head of youth
development Davie Kirkwood
believes the club is an
excellent place to start
for youngsters seeking to
progress in football.
(*Ken Macpherson*)

'Throughout every league in Scotland, including the Highland League, the number of players who have come through systems at Ross County and Inverness is frightening. We can only focus on the young, local talent because of the area we're in.'

BHOYS BELITTLED

In those far-off days of the Vikings, Dingwall was an administrative centre, a place of decision-making. For Ross County and their legions of fans on 10 April 2010, the big decisions were being taken in the Mount Florida area of Glasgow, where Derek Adams was laying out his strategy and tactics for the 12.15pm kick-off against Celtic in the semi-final of the Scottish Cup.

Celtic had won the competition 34 times. The SPL giants had also won the league championship on 42 occasions and, in 1967, they became the first British club to win the European Cup, beating Inter Milan 2–1 in the final in Portugal, when the Lisbon Lions were born.

The combination of the mass exodus to Hampden and the early kick-off brought a strange atmosphere to Dingwall, normally busy and bustling on a Saturday.

Dr Eleanor Scott, out on the streets for the Green Party in the General Election campaign, might have recognised she had picked the wrong time and the wrong place to try to win votes. Minds and people were elsewhere.

Who would have imagined that just a few weeks later, the Conservatives and the Liberal Democrats would have entered a coalition to run the country? David Cameron became the Tory Prime Minister while Nick Clegg, from the Lib Dems, was his deputy.

From 6am, a convoy of cars and as many as 30 buses, half of which were subsidised by the club, began to head south over the Kessock Bridge and on to the A9. Flags and scarves in County's dark blue colours were proudly displayed, while thousands of fans elected to don the team shirt.

Club president, Roy MacGregor, keen to mark this special day, treated 800 of his staff at Global Energy Group to a day out, providing free transport, tickets to the semi-final and a pre-match buffet at the national stadium. It was, as one member of staff pointed out, a 'fabulous gesture' and helped create a particular atmosphere among that group.

On the A9, the Dingwall division of the Staggies army was joined by recruits from Inverness, Aviemore, Kingussie and other Highland towns and villages. More mini-buses, additional cars and other coaches joined the invasion force.

Conversations turned to the performances and results in the previous rounds of the competition. Fans spoke of how County had swamped Third Division Berwick Rangers 5–1 in the third round at Victoria Park and followed this up with a 4–0 victory over Inverurie Locos from the Highland League.

The fifth round brought Stirling Albion to the UK's most northerly league

The happy atmosphere among County supporters at the semi-final against Celtic. (*Press and Journal*)

club, but they left with their tails between their legs following a 9-0 drubbing, with single goals from Alex Keddie, Richard Brittain, Stuart Kettlewell and Scott Morrison, a double from Michael Gardyne and a hat-trick from Garry Wood.

That set the scene for a visit to Edinburgh on 13 March 2010 and a quarter-final against Hibernian, riding high in the Premier League. It was to be a pulsating tie, with County producing a breathtaking draw that made the rest of Scottish football sit up and take notice.

The line-ups that day were: Hibernian: Stack, Murray, Hogg, Hanlon, Wotherspoon, McBride, Miller, Rankin (Danny Galbraith 59), Stokes (Benjelloun 59), Nish, Riordan.

Ross County: McGovern, Miller, Morrison, Boyd, Keddie, Scott, Lawson, Brittain, Vigurs, Gardyne, Barrowman.

Colin Nish's early strike for the home side might have had thoughts turning to a potential barrage of goals coming from Hibs, but parity was established on 15 minutes when a Gardyne strike was diverted into the net by Ian Murray, the Easter Road defender horrified as the ball rebounded off his chest and into the net.

Derek Riordan put Hibs back in front just before the interval, but Gardyne underlined County's second-half dominance with a strike that gave them a replay at Victoria Park on the evening of 23 March. And what a night that turned out to be.

Victoria Park was packed and the Staggies showed they were up for the

The scenes of joy in the County dressing room minutes after the win over Hibs in the replay at Victoria Park. (Ken Macpherson)

challenge, despite the first-half of this replay failing to produce any goals. The home side were caught cold less than a minute before the second-half was under way as Nish and then Sol Bamba won headers from Riordan's corner kick before Anthony Stokes beat Michael McGovern in the home goal.

It took County until 20 minutes from the end to equalise, Andy Barrowman bundling the ball home in a goalmouth scramble. It allowed the Dingwall supporters to step up their vocal support, with their heroes pushing hard for a win to underline their greater possession.

Remarkably, it came in the dying moments of this absorbing replay. Graeme Smith, the Hibs goalkeeper, crashed into a team-mate as he went for Richard Brittain's corner kick. It left Scott Boyd clear at the back post and he sent the ball into the net to spark the most memorable of celebrations as Brian Winter, the referee, blew the final whistle a matter of seconds later.

Hundreds of Ross County supporters flooded the pitch, all anxious to congratulate their heroes while moments later, in the home dressing room and in the boardroom, there were hugs and back-slaps at the realisation that the Staggies had achieved something special—a place in the semi-final against Celtic, a tie worth £250,000 to the Highlanders.

The County team that clear, crisp March night was: McGovern, Miller, Morrison, Boyd, Keddie, Scott, Lawson (Wood 63), Brittain, Vigurs, Gardyne (Kettlewell 90), Barrowman (Craig 75).

Derek Adams and his directors took a sharp intake of breath as they realised the enormity of the achievement. It was a remarkable result and performance against SPL high-flyers, but it was to pale into comparative insignificance with what was to come a few weeks later.

For Neil Lennon, acting manager of the Hoops and a young coach keen to make his mark in the wake of the departure of the ineffectual Tony Mowbray, whose managerial reign at Celtic Park lasted less than a season, it was an opportunity to lead his charges to the Cup final and stake his claim for the job on a permanent basis.

County had reached that stage of the competition courtesy of a string of eye-catching results and performances, starting with that 5–1 third round home win over Berwick Rangers on 28 November 2009. Would this sunny day in Glasgow signal the end of the Scottish Cup journey on which they had embarked less than five months earlier?

Derek Adams had no intention of 'sitting-in' against a side that was second in the Premier League. What was there to lose? No-one really expected anything other than a Celtic victory – though Adams was not among them – and a place in the final against either Dundee United or Raith Rovers, scheduled to play their semi-final at Hampden the following day.

Adams opted for a positive approach to the task in hand. This was his team selection that sunny afternoon: McGovern, Miller, Morrison, Boyd, Keddie, Scott, Brittain, Vigurs, Gardyne (Lawson 90), Barrowman, Craig.

Those who remained on the bench were, Malin, Kettlewell, Di Giacomo and Wood.

Celtic's line-up as they tried to salvage a season having conceded that they could not catch Rangers in the league, was: Zaluska, Hinkel (Rasmussen 84), Naylor, Thompson, O'Dea, N'Guemo (Crosas 42), Brown, McGeady, Keane, Samaras, Fortune (McCourt 67). The substitutes who did not participate were Cervi and Wilson.

The scene was set before 24,535 spectators and as referee Willie Collum started the game, the atmosphere was highly charged.

Adams had been manager for three years following a spell as player-coach but, at just 34 years old, he was still a rookie in this role. Could he handle such a big occasion, such a huge moment in the history of the First Division club?

Before the tie, he reminded the world that he had someone alongside him with immense experience, a man he could trust. He was, of course, referring to his father, George, of whom he said: 'We have our arguments, but we'll fight one another's battles. If he wasn't on my side then something would be wrong.

'You always think you're going to win the next game. We believed that when we went to Hibs in the quarter-final and in the replay against them. Can we win a semi-final against Celtic? I'm under no illusions about how difficult a test it is. However, you've got to have belief.

'Look, it's still 11 versus 11. I was at Motherwell when we beat the Old Firm when the likes of Henrik Larsson were playing.

'It's about how we adapt to the situation. When I played Celtic with Motherwell, we wanted to prove a point. They were better than us but that doesn't mean you can't beat them. It's about your own game and closing down your opponent.

'I played with some great players at Motherwell, it was a great group, and it's very similar at County.

'We also have ability in our squad and beating Hamilton in the League

ROSS COUNTY

From Highland League to Hampden

Overleaf.
County fans cheer on their team against Celtic.
(*Ken Macpherson*)

75

A stunning goal from Steven Craig sends Celtic reeling. (*Ken Macpherson*)

Cup then going on to do well against Dundee United in that competition gave us confidence.

'We then had two games against Hibs and the players did so well in both matches. There is a great feeling of confidence here now.'

Those were optimistic words before this important game against such powerful opponents, but that belief was never more evident than during the semi-final and the men from Ross-shire did what they said they would, they took the game to their opponents, stretching the Celtic defence and provoking frustration and anger in equal measure from Lennon.

When Steven Craig outpaced the Hoops defence early in the second-half with a scything run and raced in on goal, his finish to beat Lukasz Zaluska, the Celtic goalkeeper, was a breathtaking strike. It was only what County deserved. The goal raised the level of excitement and expectation among the happy Highland throng.

Martin Scott's late goal clinched the win and County's first major final, and when the whistle was blown for full-time a few minutes later, it was the cue for a Highland party to begin, both at Hampden and 200 miles away in Dingwall, where the streets suddenly came to life. With radio and television reporters relaying the news worldwide, there were undoubted celebrations among

Highlanders in various parts of the planet, proud to hear of one of football's most dramatic giant-killing acts.

Steven Craig, faced by a prodding microphone, hailed his manager as another Jose Mourinho, and said there were County players who believed they owed him a debt of gratitude for preserving their careers.

'He's made some wayward decisions,' Craig told sportswriters in the heat of the moment, 'but they've worked.

'The gaffer's very modest. He won't take any credit. That's what the boys like about him.'

Lennon's disappointment was palpable. Hadn't his frustrations boiled over as he watched his under-performing side? Hadn't he accepted that all his encouragement from the technical area was falling on deaf ears? The stand-in Hoops boss made his feelings known when Georgios Samaras, with his lack of urgency, was caught in possession, hurling his water bottle to the ground like a baby having a tantrum.

Later, he was scathing in his criticism of his players. 'There was no desire,' he said. 'I am sick of seeing our players fall over. I am sick of seeing strikers not wanting to go in where it hurts to score a goal for the team.

'We can't keep clean sheets either, we're too soft. We don't have enough winners.'

The lacklustre Landry N'Guemo was pulled from proceedings and replaced in midfield by Marc Crosas before half-time, a manoeuvre that merely underlined the superiority of the underdogs, who had Brittain oozing composure at the centre of their side, from where he pulled the strings like a puppeteer. He and his team-mates were in control and showed no sign of surrendering it.

Robbie Keane, the striker Celtic brought in on loan from Tottenham and was earning £65,000 a week, appeared to lose interest as Alex Keddie kept him in check, the Irishman frequently taking his colleagues to task for their failure to get to grips with the game.

'Robbie Keane's a world-class player,' Keddie said after the game, 'but we tamed the beast.'

While Lennon berated his men during the interval, his counterpart in the other changing room simply had to remind his hungry pups that they were on the verge of something memorable.

Had Samaras's second-half effort gone into the County goal rather than against the post, it might all have been so different, though no-one in dark blue colours that day believed that.

'The performance was outstanding,' Derek Adams said in the immediate aftermath of the game. 'People had written us off and we deserve all the respect that we will get now. It is a massive result in Scottish football, and a magnificent day for our football club.'

He and his battling side knew, even before Andy Barrowman's cross was turned in by Scott after 88 minutes, that the day was theirs.

Adams looked to the adoring County fans in the national stadium. 'Look at them. Some of them left at 5am and they have got it all to do again in May.'

ROSS COUNTY

From Highland League to Hampden

Martin Scott connects and the ball hits the back of the Celtic net. County are in the final.
(*Ken Macpherson*)

That, he knew, would be no hardship. To a man, and woman, those fans were thankful for their team manager's guidance. Back in Dingwall, the eeriness that hung over the town would have puzzled anyone arriving there and unaware of what was happening all those miles away in Glasgow.

At 4.45pm, however, the locals were stirred into serious celebration, and it didn't take long until journalists and television crews descended on the town to record the reaction of the citizens, as news desks up and down the country demanded the story.

Shop-owner Anne Campbell had shut her premises to watch the match at the British Legion club with dozens of others.

'It is just fantastic,' she said immediately after the game. 'I feel as if I played the whole 90 minutes. Now I am going to go back and re-open the shop. It will be a party the whole week-end long, especially when the boys get back. The town is buzzing and it is only going to get better.'

Pipe Major Trevor Dear played a Highland Fling and County fans danced a jig in the street while the Mallard Bar, by the railway station, came alive after a very quiet afternoon.

Lorraine Russell, the bar supervisor, told reporters: 'We are normally very busy soon after opening, but today we hadn't seen a soul, after being open for an hour. It got busier as some people came in to watch the match.

'However, it all changed after the game, as people came in to celebrate. The whole town went crazy. It was the lull before the storm.'

On the High Street, Ladbrokes, usually queued out the door on previous Grand National days, reported one of the quietest big race days they had experienced. They had Ross County at 10–1 against a win at Hampden, though despite such generous odds, few punters would have taken advantage of them against such lofty opposition.

REACHING FOR THE TOP

When Derek Adams returned to Scotland in 1996 to resurrect his football career with Ross County, he could not have dreamt that that 14 years later, he would be managing them and leading the team into a Scottish Cup final at Hampden.

Yet, even all those years ago, despite being a strip of a lad of 21, Adams had harboured thoughts of one day following his father George into coaching and management. And when the time came, he was in good company.

'I always wanted to coach and manage at some point in my career,' he said, 'and I did my first coaching badges when I was in my 20s. It was always an idea to do that.

'I did my Uefa A licence assessment at Clyde's Broadwood ground. I was 29-years-old and I was in the referee's room.

'Sitting to my left was Terry Butcher, the former England captain, while on my right was Alan Shearer, another former England captain; two of British football's biggest names and most revered figures.

'I thought to myself, how did this young lad, born in Glasgow and brought up in Ellon and Aberdeen, come to be in this situation? They were nervous and so was I.'

Adams did his pro licence five years later, a two-year course where students take in disciplines like business management as well as a visit to a foreign club which, in his case, was AZ Alkmaar in Holland, where Ronald Koemen, the former Ajax, Barcelona and Netherlands defender and midfielder, was manager.

'I looked at their set-up, their youth academy and watched AZ against Olympiakos in the Champions League. I also visited the European under-21 championship in Sweden. You analyse the games, the coaches, their tactics, the shape of the teams, their warm-ups, their coaching methods and you try and take back what you've learned to your club.'

The would-be manager set out on the path to becoming a coach while he was still at Motherwell and continued on it when he went to Aberdeen. Between those clubs, he finished the A licence course.

He accepted that one of the problems he experienced was that he started analysing his own managers and their coaching methods, a factor that made them wary as he became older and began to try to read their thinking.

'I had a situation at Aberdeen under Jimmy Calderwood when he said to Sandy Clark, the coach: "Leave that boy Adams alone. He's too bright for us."

'On the pro licence course were other young coaches, like Steven Pressley,

Alex Rae, Chris McCart, Sandy Stewart, Terry Butcher, Derek McInnes, Scott Leitch and others; 16 in total.

'I took over at County from Dick Campbell just eight games into the Second Division campaign and I went from player to player-manager. The players at the time were great. Because I'm very organised and was quick to arrange training and formations, it helped that I knew what I was talking about.

'The club had made a decision that it wasn't working out with Dick Campbell and he left. I was caretaker manager with Davie Kirkwood and Stewart Petrie and it worked well. We got results and I was offered the position.'

But should he, at just 32-years of age, take the job? Wasn't it a step too far, too quickly? And wasn't the fact that his father was director of football going to solicit allegations of nepotism?

'I thought it was an opportunity, especially with the type of people we had, to enter management at an early age, even though I could have played on.

'I didn't feel there was a problem with my father being director of football. I'd been under a kind of pressure all my professional life with that and didn't see this job as bringing extra pressure.

'I'd been hearing those charges since my primary school days, that I was picked for the team only because of my dad. I developed a thick skin because I had to.

'I've had people talking about me getting things because of my dad since I was five years old. This was no different. I'm now 34, so these days it's not really going to worry me.

'I have the skin of a rhino and body armour of a Terminator. So I don't care what anyone says. They can have a go at whatever they want. The statistics are there for all to see. I was never going to say no to the job because of what was going to be said.'

He has a right to be defiant. After all, didn't he lead County to the Second Division title in his first season in charge? Hadn't that answered his critics?

The step from player to boss was not as dramatic as some would envisage. In short, it was a problem he refused to countenance, taking the decision to remove himself from participating in training and, instead, simply overseeing the sessions and the coaching.

'I took the responsibility,' he said, 'and I stopped playing. I felt I couldn't be on the pitch and be seen to criticise my players if I had made a bad pass or done something else wrong. That's where many player-managers go wrong. I haven't played a first-team match since.'

The Adams ethos is to treat others as you would wish to be treated and, as an admirer of the Dutch style of football, to instil in his charges the need to play a passing game. To achieve that, he had to have a group of footballers capable of adopting his way of thinking, and he assembled a squad of technique and athleticism on the tightest of budgets.

But how did this young man from a middle-class background and raised in the leafy west end of Aberdeen, the oil capital of Europe, integrate into the sometimes rough-tough world of football? Was his lack of swagger and arrogance a hindrance in the dressing rooms of Motherwell, Aberdeen and Ross County?

'It may have been,' he said. 'I've never been blasé. I've always treated people properly. If somebody crosses me, I let them off once. The second time it is history.

'I have respect for people and I get on well with others. I also treat the players with respect and if they're good for me, I'll give them it back ten-fold. I am strong-minded, however, and I like things done the way I want them to be done.'

Adams also insists on good behaviour from his players and has a knack of relaying such a requirement from them, with the normal industrial language of the training ground frowned upon.

'I like my players to be presentable,' he insisted. 'I don't have any time for swearing, though I know it happens. It is occasionally mentioned that they have to watch what they're saying and how they behave when representing the club.

'I'm not naive. I'm aware swearing goes on, but it is all about acting responsibly. The players understand my feelings. I don't swear in the dressing room and that filters through to them. There are ways of making them understand.'

Ross County's budget for on-field activities is never far from Derek Adams' thoughts. Indeed, it may be argued that his skills with finances is on a par with his ball juggling ability as he casts an envious eye in the direction of other clubs in the First Division, clubs who have failed to come close to County's success.

'We were never in the position of winning the First Division title because of our budget. Our aim in 2009–10 was to improve on the previous season. And finishing in the top half of the league and reaching a major cup final for the first time in the club's history satisfied that requirement.

'We also went to the semi-final of the Challenge Cup and we beat Hamilton Academical, from the Premier League, 2–1 in the second round of the Co-operative Insurance Cup. Ross County will probably never have a better season.

'The only improvement would come if they make the SPL and at this stage, that process is in place, but the finances to make the squad better would have to be significantly increased.

'In the 2009–10 season, we had a third of Dundee's budget, half of Inverness Caley Thistle's, and lower than that of Dunfermline, Queen of the South, Partick Thistle and of Morton.'

Rudyard Kipling's words, 'if you can meet with triumph and disaster and treat those two imposters just the same' might have been composed for Derek Adams. In the wake of the glorious results against Hibernian and Celtic, there was no flag-waving, no draping himself in a Ross County scarf, no triumphalism nor histrionics. It's simply not his way.

Indeed, in the immediate aftermath of the semi-final victory over Celtic, his words were calm, measured, and critical.

ROSS COUNTY

From Highland League to Hampden

'Football puts you under pressure all the time, game to game,' he said. 'You might get a high, but you know you'll also get a kick in the teeth some time.

'We were unfortunate not to beat Hibernian at Easter Road but, despite many people writing us off, we raised our standards for the replay and it was a great performance to finish the game as we did with a last-minute header from Scott Boyd to take us through. That was a great occasion for us.

'We went to Hampden and were written off by the media and by ex-players and again we performed extremely well.

'I didn't think our chances should have been discarded after the way we had played over two games against Hibs. And we'd also played well against Hamilton and Dundee United in the Co-operative Insurance Cup.

'People were saying Celtic were already through to the final and I felt that was disrespectful. They could have said Celtic were favourites. I could have accepted that, but not that it was a foregone conclusion.

'It didn't read right to me and we had to prove a point.

'I translated that message to my players through the media. Players read what is written in the newspapers and that's a big way of ensuring they know my thoughts.'

Adams recognised, the night before the tie against Celtic, that the mood in his camp was restrained, but confident.

The Staggies were housed in the Westerwood Hotel in Cumbernauld and had a quiet meal. The players were bubbly, happy and were chatting non-stop.

On the morning of the game, they were laughing and joking and he could see they were not fazed with what lay before them. He began to realise something special, and dramatic, was achievable.

'At Hampden, our fans were waving their flags and their scarves and the atmosphere was electric,' he recalled.

'I had played there many times and scored a goal for Motherwell against Rangers in a Scottish Cup semi-final. Lots of our boys had not experienced Hampden; the big lockers in the dressing rooms, the size of those dressing rooms, the other changing room for the officials and staff and the feeling of soaking up the sense of occasion, which started with motorbike outriders giving us a police escort from our hotel.'

But, if there was a game of football to be won, psychology would have its part to play. The question was: who would win the battle of minds?

'I remember seeing Neil Lennon at the start of the game standing in the technical area at the side of the pitch,' he added, 'and I decided to remain in my area in the Hampden dugout, which is a few steps up from the track and away from the playing surface.

'In the first ten minutes, I went to the side of the pitch once. Celtic were struggling and Lennon started to look towards his own dugout I think for advice from someone, perhaps Johan Mjallby, his assistant. He was clearly worried.

'I knew if I went down to the side of the pitch, adjacent to where he was standing, it would ease the pressure on him. It was psychology. He was alone down there and I left him there, apart from a couple of visits.

ROSS COUNTY

From Highland League to Hampden

Opposite.
Mind games at Mount Vernon. Adams remains calm as Neil Lennon urges on his side. (*Ken Macpherson*)

85

'The players get a feeling that, if the manager is standing there all the time, shouting and bawling, then he's apprehensive.'

Going in at the break still on level terms and without having conceded a goal, Adams issued a warning that their opponents would raise the tempo as soon as the whistle to re-start the match was blown.

'I asked my players if they enjoyed coming to Hampden, the police escort, the importance of the occasion. Did they like the attention and the love of the fans? And the last thing I said before we went out for the second half was: If you liked all of that, then believe. If you want to come back again for the final, then go out and perform and win the game.'

Whatever chutzpah those men in dark blue had after their more than competent opening 45 minutes was boosted even further by those simple words, spoken with conviction and feeling, from a young coach whose belief that victory was not only possible but probable.

'I could see we had a team that wanted to win. And the best bit of the day was after Martin Scott's goal, our second, two minutes from the end. There were three minutes of added-on time, which meant we had five minutes in all to take on board that we were through to the Scottish Cup final. It was a relief. We knew we were there and that gave the fans, the coaching staff and the players enjoyment beyond belief. It was a fantastic occasion for us.'

Adams had signed around 90 per cent of the squad, players he had hand-picked and who were willing to accept wages ranging from £400 to £600, petty-cash to those who operate in the upper echelons of football in the UK and beyond. He believed in them and they knew that, but there is often a difficult balance to be struck in order to convey who is in charge, who is responsible for producing results.

'You can't be too critical of them,' he conceded, 'but you also have a way to explain where they are going wrong and tell them when they are doing well.

'You have to be assertive. You have to be the boss, but you have to look after them because they are the ones who have to go on to the park and do the business for you. They are part of you. They are no different from you. It's just that you are the leader off the park and you have to show you can lead them. That may come in many ways: how you act, your appearance, what you say in the media. They do take things from that.'

Old school football managers may take the view that it is unimportant to be liked by their team, that a lack of popularity in the dressing room doesn't matter. It is an assertion with which Derek Adams disagrees.

'There is no doubt that it's important to be liked,' he said. 'I played with the majority of my squad, either at Ross County, at Livingston or at Aberdeen. So, they know what I was like before and if they have a feeling for you, they'll play for you.'

Scott Boyd, Gary Miller, Martin Scott and Richard Brittain all played at Livingston with him while he, Steven Craig and Scott Morrison were team-mates at Aberdeen, and he played alongside Andy Barrowman and Alex Keddie at Ross County. Knowing and liking each other, then, has clearly worked well for the Staggies.

*Opposite.
County's Gary Miller and
Martin Scott ensure Celtic's
Aiden McGeady is kept in
check. (Ken Macpherson)*

Of course, the role of the modern-day football manager doesn't start on the training pitch and end on the day of a game. There are additional tasks, some managers label as irritants and side issues which get in the way of the job – dealing with the media.

The bigger the occasion, as County have discovered this season, the greater the attention of the national newspapers, television stations and radio broadcasters.

There are pre-match interviews, previews of games, feature articles and post-match questions and assessments. It can be a strenuous affair, which some team bosses handle badly while others, like Adams, perform well.

He remembered the immediate aftermath of that Scottish Cup semi-final victory, trying to savour the moment while satisfying the needs of microphone-wielding radio and TV reporters, all looking for their sound bites.

'I was on the park at Hampden for 20 minutes after the final whistle,' he added, 'doing radio and television interviews.

'But before being whisked off to the media room for the post-match press conference, I pleaded to be allowed to visit the dressing room for a couple of minutes. I had to gather my thoughts before I spoke with the press. I always prepare what I am to say and how it is going to come across. Some things you say you know will have consequences. You have to deal with them, as long as you know your comments are right.

'I went into the dressing room and went round the players and staff. We couldn't believe what we had just achieved. That was a great feeling; taking players, staff, supporters – and myself – to Hampden and being rewarded for our belief. It was the magnitude of the result and how we performed.'

Derek Adams is nothing if not grounded. Family is important to him, and to them, which is why his mother and sister have been ever-present spectators during his playing and managing career.

'They go to every Ross County game,' he is proud to proclaim, 'and they've had to deal with the pressure, not only of me being a player but of my father being involved, too.

'He went to Motherwell as head of youth development when I was already there, then I went to Ross County when he was in place as director of football. So, that's a pressure. I know there have been questions asked and criticisms made and it affects others, but that's where your family have got to be supportive and strong and I was pleased those days at Hampden were great for them.'

ROSS COUNTY

From Highland League to Hampden

County 'keeper Michael McGovern celebrates beating his former club, Celtic. (*Press & Journal*)

THE ASSISTANT:
BEEN THERE, DONE THAT

It was in February 2009 that Craig Brewster, keen as ever to keep himself fit, approached Derek Adams to request access to training facilities. After all, he had never known a period during a long and distinguished playing career when he hadn't experienced the daily routine of physical exercise.

Only a month had elapsed since Inverness Caledonian Thistle sacked him as they slumped to the basement of the Premier League. It was not a happy time for the tall Dundonian, whose playing career took him from Forfar Athletic to Raith Rovers, where he formed a successful striking partnership with Gordon Dalziel that helped the Kirkcaldy club to the First Division Championship.

In 1993, he returned to Dundee United, where he had been discarded as a schoolboy, and after a slow start to life in the SPL he scored the winning goal in the 1994 Scottish Cup final against Rangers.

Two years later, when his contract expired and he was keen to sample life and football abroad, he joined the Greek club Ionikos, where he became a huge favourite with the fans during his five years there.

'I thoroughly enjoyed my time in Greece,' he says. 'Greek football clubs have always been able to attract players from abroad and the wealthy owners often pay the top players' wages out of their own pocket. In Scotland, we do everything by the book but there, club presidents can pay players' salaries and they are always keen to make big signings every season.

'Greek football was good for me, in terms of what it taught me about tactics, diet and fitness. The Greek league is not as intense as here. The SPL is full-on for 90 minutes. There is a slower tempo in Greece and it is about possession.'

Brewster's return to Scotland in 2001 saw him join Hibernian, where his experience and expertise helped the development of his young striker partner, Garry O'Connor. His move to Dunfermline a year later brought him alongside Stevie Crawford and together they became one of the most feared and formidable front partnerships in Scotland.

A successful time as Inverness Caley's player-manager resulted in Dundee United offering him a similar role with his former club, but it ended unhappily with the Tannadice side slipping into the lower reaches of the SPL and their young boss being shown the door after a miserable period.

Still fit and equipped for football at a high level, he joined Aberdeen and, despite dislocating his shoulder and being unable to play for some months, he returned to the Dons side. Belying his 41 years was a testament to a career of looking after himself and retaining his fitness.

Opposite.
Adams with his able and experienced lieutenant Craig Brewster. (*Ken Macpherson*)

Overleaf.
Andy Barrowman fires in a shot, despite the attention of Josh Thomson and Andeas Hinkel. (*Press & Journal*)

He returned to Caley Thistle as manager in August 2007 but was sacked in January 2009.

'It was the following month that I asked Derek if I could train with his players for a couple of days each week,' he explains, 'and he not only agreed but offered me a player-coach role. I did that until the end of the season and in the summer he asked me to become his assistant, which I was delighted to accept.

'We had a relatively small group of players – 19 – until January and then Derek brought two more in. The season was very positive and, of course, the run in the Scottish Cup where we were fortunate to get a couple of home ties was exciting.

'We hit nine goals past Stirling Albion only to be drawn against Hibs at Easter Road. Everyone expected us to be beaten, but we put on a performance that was exceptional and we took a 2–2 draw to take them back to Dingwall for a replay.

'Many thought our chance had gone, but again we put on another super display to win. In both games we had to come back and the last minute winner at Victoria Park in the replay that night was very sweet.'

Brewster's recollection of the Scottish Cup semi-final will live with him for a long time. County were acutely aware that Celtic's form was not as good as they were capable of, although they knew Neil Lennon, handed the job of interim manager after the sacking of Tony Mowbray, would lift the Hoops, just as he'd done in the handful of SPL games in which he'd been in charge.

'But we believed that if we played anything like we'd done against Hibs, we could give them a fright,' says the County assistant manager, 'though even against a Celtic team struggling with confidence, it was still a tall order. The players, however, were up for it and our performance that day surprised a few people and shocked others, though not us.

'Steven Craig's opener was a stunning goal and even standing on the touchline we never felt the team was under any real, sustained pressure from Celtic. All right, Georgios Samaras had a good chance – probably the chance of the game – then Robbie Keane had a header that went by the post, followed by an attempt on goal from Marc-Antoine Fortune.

'So, three chances they had, and against good Celtic teams you can be steamrollered. That never happened.

'I didn't realise our second goal, from "Jimmy" Scott, had come so late on and the result reverberated around the world because of the huge following Celtic have.

'Ross County, the players and the manager were talked about everywhere. It sent shock waves through the football world.

'You can also see and feel things happening and developing in a game, and in the first-half our side was confident and keen to take the ball.

'Playing against Celtic and Rangers, you need to be strong physically and mentally and we were certainly strong psychologically. They were full of energy, full of running and when you come in at half-time not having conceded, you know you have real chance.

'We knew how we started the second-half would be important. If we gave the ball away too quickly then our opponents would get a grip of the game. They never did. We didn't allow that to happen because when we did have the ball, we kept it and we made them work rather than the other way round.

'There was a hunger, a desire to say "I want this", and that's despite the fact that our lads earn a fraction of the Celtic players' wages. You have to make things happen.'

Brewster's views on how to mould a group of players, who have either failed to make the grade elsewhere, some with bigger clubs, or who were discarded at too early an age when they might have been late developers, into a unit capable of beating the best sides in the land are straightforward.

'First and foremost, you have to have a good manager. And then the mentality of the squad has to be good, as does a long list of items to bring the best out of players. It isn't easy. Nor is it easy to get them to do it consistently.

'The atmosphere in the dressing room before the semi-final didn't produce any more nerves from our players than normal because all the expectations were on Celtic. That's the difference in football. The tough part is when you have to live up to the expectations, but it just shows you what can happen when you have 11 players on the park bursting a gut.

'Of course, you have to have talent and other attributes. You have to have a lot of things, but you have to have the mental strength. That is so important.

'Lennon said we deserved the win and that's credit to him. He was right, of course, although he might not have criticised his players the way he did had he been the manager and not the acting manager.

'He might still have had a go at them, but maybe not in such a full-on way. Sometimes, though, you have to be brutally honest. The fans are looking for honesty.

'From Ross County's point of view, our road to the final was a great story.'

ROSS COUNTY

From Highland League to Hampden

FROM DINGWALL
TO THE DEEP SOUTH

The story and character of the man whose name is inextricably linked with the Highlands and Ross County is probably best summed up by a line in a newspaper in the late 1960s.

'There are only two Rolls Royces in Memphis, Tennessee,' the *Press & Journal* reported in a diary item, 'one belongs to Elvis Pressley, the other to Frank Thomson.'

Charismatic and colourful, Thomson is still revered by the people of Ross-shire half a century after he had swept them up with a mixture of passion and chutzpah.

Thomson made an impact wherever he went. Players, young and old, could not have failed to have been impressed and influenced by the strength of his personality and his 'can do' approach to everything in which he became involved.

He pledged to haul Ross County out of their mediocrity and to make them a talking point in the Highland League, hence the recruitment of quality signings from league football: Sammy Wilson, Jack Lornie and Jim Hosie, all of whom featured elsewhere in these pages.

They were to bring new meaning to the club and offer the supporters in and around the town of Dingwall real hope that their team would win their first ever Highland League title.

Thomson's time was the era ushered in by the Beatles, James Bond and *Dr No*, and John F Kennedy. It was an exciting period, as attitudes changed and in Britain there were entrepreneurs ready to promote themselves and their ideas.

He wanted his company Invergordon Distillers, formed in 1961, on the map.

Invergordon town takes its name from an eighteenth-century laird, Sir William Gordon. The Cromarty Firth is one of the best deep-water harbours in Europe and was an important commercial port and naval base. The distillery was commissioned in 1959 to create employment in the area following the departure of the Royal Navy.

The Ben Wyvis malt distillery was built within the grain distillery complex in 1965 and one of Thomson's marketing ideas was to assemble the finest pipe band he could and fashion them into world champions. And so the Invergordon Distillery Pipe Band was formed.

He hand-picked the best pipers and drummers he could find, offered them work with his company and gave them as much time as they needed to practice within the eight-acre site of the distillery on the northern shore of the Cromarty Firth, an area with some of the best arable land in Scotland.

Arguably, his biggest signing was Alex Duthart, described by one of Ross County's former players under Thomson as 'the Denis Law of drummers.'

Duthart was to become a leading player in the theatre of dreams his new boss was keen to create, as he saw the band as a key marketing and public relations tool that would help him crack the American market… if they became world champions.

ROSS COUNTY

*From Highland League
to Hampden*

Frank Thomson

How could they fail? Hadn't he brought together the best pipers and drummers, poached from other leading bands?

Duthart was an interesting character. Born in 1925 in the village of Cambusnethan, near Wishaw, Lanarkshire, he took up drumming around the age of eight, taught by his father who at that time was a noted figure in pipe band drumming in his own area.

Alex was just 12 when he joined his first band, Craigneuk Parish Church Juvenile Pipe Band. A shortage of drums meant that, at first, he walked beside the band, but he went on to play both bass drum and snare drum.

He progressed over the years, becoming more and more proficient, and winning many solo drumming competitions until he felt the need to step aside to give others a chance.

Duthart also played with local big bands in ballrooms in Hamilton and Glasgow, but he was coaxed back to pipe bands in 1957 with the famous Shotts and Dykehead Caledonia Pipe Band, putting together a new drum corps and helping steer them to win that year's World Drumming Championship.

His 29-year stay with that band was interrupted by a two-year spell with Frank Thomson's newly-formed Invergordon Distillery Pipe Band, presumably because the millionaire from the north made it worth his while.

Jim Hosie, himself encouraged to take the road to the Highlands as part of the Ross County team that won the Highland League championship in 1967, remembers the band well.

'The band members all had jobs in the maintenance department at the distillery,' he said, 'although most of the time they spent practising, trying to fulfil Thomson's dream.

'They were wonderful, but so good that they became a victim of their own excellence. The judges of pipe band competitions are seated inside a tent from where they are not allowed to see which band is performing. It allows them to judge on the quality of the musicianship alone.

'But the drums always gave it away. They knew instantly, because of how good the drummers were, which band they were listening to and who the drum major was, and were marked down. It was like they were handicapped.

'Thomson's dream never materialised, and slowly the band disappeared.'

With his goatee beard and astrakhan hat, Thomson was a colourful character and a visionary who saw great things for the Cromarty Firth – a deep-sea port, oil refineries and other industrial developments.

He wanted success with whatever he touched or helped to fund, whether it was the pipe band or Ross County FC.

He had a presence and enjoyed being spotted in his Rolls Royce. He was always ready to promote the area in which he lived and worked, proclaiming it would provide an example of business and industrial development for the rest of British industry and the world.

Interestingly, he was described by Magnus Linklater in *The Times*, in the wake of County's Scottish Cup semi-final win over Celtic, as a 'rough diamond businessman with a finger in many pies, not all of them savoury.'

On one LP record – Pipes in Concert – the distillery band issued in 1966, a track featured three marches: Frank Thomson, John Gordon of Drummuie, and General Collingwood's Farewell to Scottish Command. It would no doubt have done wonders for their founder's ego.

No chronicle of Ross County would be complete without recording the influence of this tall, bearded Aberdeen accountant-cum-entrepreneur, whose style was matched by substance as he knitted himself into the fabric of the sporting and business communities of the north of Scotland.

Thomson gravitated to the Highlands from his native Aberdeen in 1951 and in time morphed from accountant to visionary and showman ready to transform the economic fortunes of the area with his determined approach to business and desire to create jobs.

Never known to shy away from a reporter's notebook, nor a photographer's Hasselblad, Thomson rose to prominence in the 1960s.

It was in 1961 that he opened the Invergordon Distillery, the largest grain distillery in Europe, which employed 400 local people.

His profile rose significantly when he mounted the MacPuff campaign to save the Inverness to Kyle rail link from the axe of Dr Beeching, the British Railways boss, who cut 4,000 route miles of rail track in 1966, followed by a further 2,000 miles – 3,200km – by the end of the decade, devastating communities throughout Britain.

The campaign was to prove successful and it propelled Thomson into the public eye as a champion of the region and its people.

'We were determined to fight rationally, on economic grounds, without the mish-mash of sentiment,' he said at the time. 'Trying to keep the Kyle-Thurso lines on purely social grounds would have looked as if we were begging.

'And we succeeded. Our actions wakened up the Scottish Council for Development and Industry, and the press. In six weeks, 16 farmers and businessmen, who first met in an Invergordon hotel, had forced a Downing Street confrontation between a representative group of Scottish interests and the Prime Minister, Minister of Transport and Secretary of State for Scotland, leading the fight for north Scotland transport to a point where it affected the entire outlook of Scottish national transport generally.

'MacPuff was an activist group and we suspended our work following the appointment of Highland and Islands Development Board to lend that body our support,' Thomson said.

These were exciting and vibrant times. Thomson had become a nationally-known figure through a campaign that offered hope to other communities threatened by the Beeching cuts.

By then, he had also become chairman of Ross County, having been appointed a director in 1959. It was a role he was to relish, and the strength of his personality galvanised support as he set out to try to lead them to the Highland League championship.

Eager to put the club and, some would say himself, on the map, he pledged he would not shave until the Dingwall side registered six wins in a row. A 4–2 victory over Forres Mechanics was their sixth successive triumph, which took the team to sixth position in the league table and to mark the occasion, he

presented every player who had appeared in any of the league games with a miniature silver cup. But, as the press sought the story of the big shave, Thomson decided he rather liked his beard and it remained, becoming, along with his astrakhan hat and his maroon Rolls Royce, trademarks of this interesting and intriguing character.

According to newspaper reports at the time, it was his intervention that saved County when, along with business partner, Hugh Ryan, he kept it alive 'when it was very much in the red' by floating it as a limited company.

A strict teetotaller, he saw potential wealth in the setting up of Invergordon Distillers, where he came to know every employee by name. It was 1961 and it launched a purple patch for him as a champion of the Highlands.

There were frequent newspaper stories on this man about whom everybody was talking. In one profile of him in the *Press & Journal* of 14 March 1965, there is the tale of him joining the Army at the end of the Second World War and being sent to the War Office selection board for officer training.

'Being a socialist led me to trouble,' he recalled in that article. 'I was very left wing and obviously gave them the wrong answers. So they sent me to a psychiatrist, who put a few questions to me. He must have been satisfied because I was told I was being commissioned. I was interested in economics and landed in the Royal Army Pay Corps. I was probably the most undisciplined officer they ever had.'

There is a clear sense in researching this remarkable man that he was never happier than when at the centre of issues and, sometimes, controversies, and that he enjoyed the profile afforded him, often in high places, because of his daring style of doing business.

In 1967, for instance, having led Ross County to their first Highland League championship, bankrolling Sammy Wilson's vision and determination to raise the standard of football at the club with the introduction of better players, he produced a shock.

Morton had just won the Second Division title and Thomson accepted an invitation from the Greenock club's director/manager Hal Stewart to join their board.

Trilby-wearing Stewart was, like his old friend, a larger-than-life figure who, when announcing the appointment of his new director, proclaimed: 'Next season, Morton will be chasing Rangers and Celtic for honours. Our aim is to take the club into Europe.

'I have big plans for the future of the club and Mr Thomson will be a big asset as a director.'

Thomson, perhaps warming to the chance of richer publicity pickings in the central belt, proclaimed he would fly from Inverness to Glasgow then be driven to Greenock for Morton's home games.

The switch of clubs occurred as County's finances came under the spotlight, though Thomson, by then also the owner of Ross-shire Engineering in Dingwall, assured supporters there was no need for concern. He left his wife Sheena on the County board to retain links with the club and claimed he could be of service to both the Staggies and Morton.

In a sweeping statement he said: 'I cannot go into detail about the link-up between the two clubs. This move in the Highlands will give closer opportunity of reaching First Division football.' County were then £6,000 in the red – £77,000 in 2010 terms.

But this was a turbulent period for Thomson. His part-time appointment as a member of the Highlands and Islands Development Board was tinged with scandal over loans it had approved for companies he owned.

It became a major story with questions asked in the House of Commons over what was clearly viewed by the opposition Conservative Party as dodgy dealings.

There was turbulence, too, over his drive to establish a giant £50 million petro-chemical plant in Invergordon, with suggestions that the American oil company, Occidental, would operate it.

His link to such a venture was questioned because of his £1,200-a-year membership of the HIDB quango, with the Tories hinting that he was using his position to improve his own finances.

Willie Ross, Labour's Secretary of State for Scotland, was forced to defend Thomson and the HIDB in the Commons over this and applications from Thomson companies for government loans. In light of the difficulties it brought the minister, he was forced to announce that 'in future when a member declares a pecuniary interest in an application for financial assistance, the board will consult me as Secretary of State before granting it.' Ross would not have liked to have been placed in such a position.

Thomson's flamboyance, however, was unaffected. As mentioned elsewhere in the book, he had assembled a grade one pipe band under Pipe Major Donald Ramsay, who penned a tribute to his boss called simply, 'Frank Thomson'.

He succeeded Sir John Hunt as rector of Aberdeen University in 1967, beating off the challenge of Sir Dugald Baird and the actor Andrew Cruickshank.

But with fiscal pressures mounting, Ross-shire Engineering failed and, caught in the centre of a political storm, Thomson resigned from Highlands and Islands Development Board.

'I can hold my head high against any criticisms and can stand, with impunity, all the gossip that they fling at me because the truth will out in the end,' were his defiant words to newsmen.

Did he have any pecuniary interest in the proposed petro-chemical complex?

'I have stepped out from any situation whereby I could be accused of having a direct or indirect pecuniary interest in the Invergordon situation,' he said, though he admitted he would have accepted a major position in running it had the dream come true.

Ross said he felt Thomson played his part with the genuine well-being of the Highlands in mind. 'I have more than a feeling that someone was out to destroy the board,' said Ross of those Conservatives never enamoured by the HIDB.

ROSS COUNTY

From Highland League to Hampden

To underline that he did not always walk hand in hand with success, a travel agency business he owned in Inverness was sold and that year he was appointed president of the travel division of Holiday Inns in Memphis. The United States of America was about to experience this man who could teach another resident of the Tennessee town something about marketing and public relations. There would have been plenty of people who would not have been surprised had he announced some kind of deal with Elvis.

He was still a frequent visitor to the Highlands, however, and to his home in Strathpeffer, each time being targeted by local journalists eager to hear the latest chapter in this man's exciting life.

He had bought a ten-bedroomed house 'with air conditioning and central heating and a swimming pool being built,' so that his wife and four children could join him.

Later, on another trip home, he announced he was moving to Kentucky to start, not only his own Bourbon distillery, but to import Scotch.

In November 1967, newspapers reported that: 'The only woman director in Highland League football, Sheena Thomson, has resigned from the board of Ross County. There was no rift or quarrel with the club.'

It was all because of pressure of business, Sheena insisted, though strangely her decision to quit was given to player-coach Ian McNeill. She asked him to pass her decision on to the board. It severed a ten-year connection with the club and the Thomson family.

A move to Australia followed Frank Thomson's American adventure and he became senior adviser to the government of New South Wales, where he also took his Bourbon-distilling skills and owned a development agency that assisted in the creation and development of worker-owned and controlled businesses.

Frank Thomson died in Sydney, Australia, on 28 December 1989. He was 62. Once a staunch member of the Labour Party, he had become disenchanted with it because it had not held to its progressive and radical course.

'Anyone who is a Scot is a nationalist,' he said on one occasion in the late 1960s, 'but regionalism is what they want. I have great respect for Billy Wolfe and Arthur Donaldson [two senior figures in the SNP] as against those who climbed on the SNP bandwagon like Ludovic Kennedy and Magnus Magnusson. My nationalism doesn't lean as far as to break up a well-tried institution as the UK, but I am for more devolution.'

Thomson's far-reaching vision was a major factor in why a range of people, from the ordinary man in the street to the captains of Highland industry, believed in him.

In May 1990, after a memorial service at St Joseph's Church in his beloved Invergordon, Thomson's ashes were scattered in the sea opposite the Invergordon distillery, an act in which Don MacMillan, a former employee of the businessman and Ross County player, played a key part.

It was Frank Thomson's last wish.

'He was a great character,' said MacMillan. Those touched by Thomson's charm and personality would find no disagreement with that assessment.

CHRISTIAN VALUES
AND SPORTING HISTORY

Roy MacGregor will never be heard preaching about the Christian values he holds dear, but they're there; they always have been. His values are those of his parents, his wife Morag and of his late father-in-law, a Free Church minister.

There is, however, an admission of going off the rails at one point, though details are not forthcoming. 'Let's just say I was a bit of a rebel and I couldn't control my life,' he says.

Attempting to delve into the recesses of his mind in order to glean a modicum of intelligence about past indiscretions and misdemeanours are met with resistance.

How, then, did the conversion from rebel to Christian come about? And wasn't his refusal to attend a Scottish Cup tie between his beloved Ross County and Rangers on a Sunday indicative of the behaviour of an archetypal member of the Free Church?

It was not the big deal the media made of it, he insisted. His decision to stay away from the game was not taken so he might make a point about his religion – he is also a member of a Christian fellowship – but simply a statement that attending a football match on the Sabbath did not fit in with his beliefs.

'I have no narrow perspective,' he said. 'I'm a people person. I want the best for everyone. I have a love for people and I would like to help them improve.'

Surely, though, a man overseeing a business empire covering 23 companies and employing thousands of people must be an autocrat for it all to work?

'I hope I lead by example,' he said, 'and I take the view that people will believe in you if you do that.

'I try to be consistent with people and put myself in their shoes before I make a decision. I need them to convince me that their view is different from mine and if they do, I will change my mind.

'To get the best out of people you have to believe in them. If you're autocratic, you can't believe in them.'

But MacGregor is not a man who welcomes news of problems, unless the bearer of such bad tidings adds the caveat that a solution is at hand. If he's paying top dollar for expertise, he reckons, he doesn't need saddled with difficulties that are insurmountable.

'If there is a problem, I want them to tell me how they're going to sort it and I'll tell them if I agree.

'But I won't carry it out… you carry it out. So, don't come and put the problem on my shoulders. You deal with it.

'That carries right the way through my life.'

If MacGregor is not quite Frank Thomson incarnate, his vision is certainly in line with the man who had such an influence on the Highlands over two decades and more.

An industrialist with leanings towards culture, he wants more physical education in primary schools and more money from government for sport and the arts.

'It's about developing people,' he proclaimed. 'We don't value sport and culture enough in this country.

'If you asked people if they would pay an extra 2p in the £ to have free sport for all, and five hours a week of PE for primary schoolchildren, or more art for youngsters, they would pay it.

'It's about our responsibility and people can't see the difference. Let people understand where their money goes. We need to make a difference.'

MacGregor pointed to Frank Thomson and the difference he made to the Highlands, bringing employment, generating wealth, and giving a great deal back to the community he grew to love.

'Thomson was an interesting man,' he said. 'In many ways he changed the distilling industry. He changed it from being a small one to a big one.

'In that 1966–67 period as a young footballer, I used to thumb a lift to the football from Invergordon High Street and my lift would be either from Jim Hosie or Don MacMillan or Frank's Rolls Royce.

'He had a maroon Silver Shadow and he would work in the distillery till about half past one and a few of us would pile into the long, bench seat in the back of his car and he would talk about football all the way to Dingwall. The question on a Saturday was: were we going to travel in with the players, or in the luxury of Frank's Roller?

'He believed so much in Scotland, as I do. Maybe this extraordinary man was an influence on me. He had no boundaries and neither do I.

'His heart was in the Highlands. What I remember about him was his distillery, his football team, his pipe band and his vision.'

Roy MacGregor took 800 of his staff to Hampden for the Scottish Cup semi-final against Celtic and gave them a day to remember. For the final against Dundee United, he extended the invitation to 1,500 employees and booked every one of the stadium's executive boxes in order to offer them hospitality.

He paid for 2,000 primary schoolchildren from all across Ross-shire to be there – 'they are the next generation of Ross County supporters' – and invited every MP and MSP from the region, as well as all elected members of Highland Council, and the County managers from the time they entered the SFL in 1994.

He subsidised more than 100 buses for supporters and, rather as Thomson would have done, arranged for a pipe band to be on hand to stir Highland hearts.

'We wanted all of our supporters to share in this piece of history,' he said.

Those 13 words encapsulate what Ross County and the people across the Highlands mean to Roy MacGregor.

THE FINAL

There was something ecclesiastical about the moment Ross County and Dundee United emerged from the tunnel of the cathedral-like national stadium to the thunderous applause of 47,122 enthusiastic and excited fans.

For up to two hours before the 3pm kick-off, the supporters, dressed in the garish tangerine of the Taysiders and the more sombre dark blue, white and red of County, mingled around the stadium, posing for photographs, joking with each other, exchanging banter and generally having a fun time. This was a final for fans without the baggage of bile and bad feeling; a gathering of good will.

As each minute ticked by, so the momentum gathered pace and as the supporters congregated around the periphery of Hampden, the atmosphere became jollier and the excitement built. There could be no mistake; it was a special day and every single person aimed to enjoy it to the full.

This was an event, a happening that had 'I was there' running through it, the culmination of days of pre-match excitement in Dingwall, where special cakes complete with blue, red and white icing were available in the local baker's shop.

Other retailers proved inventive with their window displays to show they wanted to be part of the occasion.

The previous evening, the Celtic rock band Torridon, who had received permission from the Proclaimers – Scots twins Charlie and Craig Reid – to tweak their hit song 'I'm On My Way' to produce the official Staggies cup final effort, 'We're On Our Way', were joined by hundreds of other fans in Dingwall for a farewell flourish a joy.

The final chapter of this Highland fairytale was about to be written, as players and fans looked back on a remarkable cup run and examined how Dundee United had come to be their opponents that afternoon.

The road to the Scottish Cup final 2010 was this:

Ross County
Third Round: Ross County 5 (Di Giacomo 2, Lawson, Craig, Wood), Berwick Rangers 1.
Fourth round: Ross County 4 (Craig 2, Morrison, Miller), Inverurie Locos 0.
Fifth round: Ross County 9, (Keddie, Gardyne 2, Wood 3, Brittain (pen), Kettlewell, Morrison), Stirling Albion 0.
Quarter-finals: Hibs 2, Ross County 2 (Murray (og), Gardyne).
Replay: Ross County 2 (Wood, Boyd), Hibs 1.
Semi-finals: Celtic 0, Ross County 2 (Craig, Scott).

ROSS COUNTY

*From Highland League
to Hampden*

Dundee United

Fourth round: Partick Thistle 0, Dundee United 2 (Casalinuovo, Goodwillie).

Fifth round: St Johnstone 0, Dundee United 1 (Goodwillie).

Quarter-finals: Rangers 3, Dundee United 3 (Shala, Whittaker (og), Kovacevic).

Replay: Dundee United 1 (Robertson), Rangers 0.

Semi-finals: Dundee United 2 (Goodwillie, Webster), Raith Rovers 0.

Derek Adams and Lee Wilkie, the United centre-half forced to announce his retirement days earlier due to severe knee injuries that would no longer allow him to compete, led their teams out on to the perfect pitch. Affording Wilkie this honour was a gesture from United's manager Peter Houston that caused the feelings of both sets of supporters to erupt like Eyjafjallajokull, the Icelandic volcano whose ash clouds were creating havoc with the world's air traffic around this period. And not a single fan in the stadium would forget that magical moment shortly before 3pm on Saturday 15 May 2010 – the 125th year of the competition.

County fans gear up for the semi-final. (*Ken Macpherson*)

Branded the Active Nation Scottish Cup as part of a Scottish government initiative to promote fitness and well-being among the people of Scotland, the competition was sponsored by Willie Haughey, the millionaire boss of City Holdings and a former director of Celtic Football Club.

County, minnows from the First Division, had already disposed of big Premier League fish. Could they fulfil their dream and win the trophy? Or would United succeed in lifting the trophy for only the second time in their history?

Around 24 hours earlier, the team, kitted out in dark blue suits and club ties, left Dingwall in a blaze of glory. They had visited local schools, accepting the applause of a thousand star-struck children of the Highlands, sent on their way also by thousands of well-wishers lining the streets of the town to wave off Derek Adams and his squad.

'We'd had a training session in the morning and went to Dingwall Academy and the pupils of that and the primary school gave us a tremendous reception,' the manager said. 'Then, on to the main street and it was lined with people there to wish us luck.

'It was an astounding reaction, knowing we had the backing of the

ROSS COUNTY

*From Highland League
to Hampden*

Pupils at Dingwall Academy gather on the eve of the cup final to wish their County heroes good luck.
(*Press & Journal*)

ROSS COUNTY

*From Highland League
to Hampden*

Highlands. It was very touching. It was such a marvellous day for the people of Dingwall to see their team heading off to compete in the Scottish Cup final.

'Then, it was on to our hotel in Cumbernauld, where we had a meal and the boys had an early night, though I'm sure many of them took some time to get off to sleep.'

At 12.15pm on cup final day, the Ross County party, led by police motor-cyclists, made their way from Cumbernauld to Hampden, the tension on the team bus beginning to grow.

'On the bus we watched a DVD of the goals we had scored in the tournament,' Adams revealed, 'and there was a reaction from the players as they watched those goals going in.

'It was the finale of the season, and to walk out on to that Hampden turf with the County team, a First Division side and with a Highland League past and having moved on to that stage, was tremendous; a great feeling and a great sight to see all those flags and scarves of blue and white and the happy faces of our fans.'

The line-ups were:

Ross County (4-5-1): Michael McGovern; Gary Miller, Scott Boyd, Alex Keddie, Scott Morrison; Steven Craig (Paul Lawson 52 mins), Martin Scott (Garry Wood 80 mins), Richard Brittain, Iain Vigurs, Michael Gardyne (Paul Di Giacomo 77 mins); Andy Barrowman. Substitutes not used: Joe Malin, Stuart Kettlewell.

Dundee United (4-4-2): Dusan Pernis; Mihael Kovacevic (Keith Watson 83), Andy Webster, Garry Kenneth, Sean Dillon; Danny Swanson (Scott Robertson 73 mins), Prince Buaben, Morgaro Gomis, Craig Conway; John Daly, David Goodwillie (David Robertson 79). Substitutes not used: Steven Banks, Danny Cadamarteri.
Referee: Dougie McDonald.

There was no dispute in the assessment of the game that County didn't enjoy the best of starts and but for heroics from their central defensive pairing of Alex Keddie and Scott Boyd, both of whom made a series of telling and important interventions, Dundee United would certainly have raced to a first-half lead.

There were worrying signs for County. Their midfield was rendered impotent and the supply to the lone striker, Andy Barrowman, was snuffed out at source. Yet, going in at the break, there was still hope for the Staggies. After all, hadn't that been the scenario the previous month in the semi-final against Celtic?

'I was delighted it was goal-less at half-time,' said Adams, 'because United had opportunities and we hadn't started the game well. Throughout the first-half, we didn't play anything like we could.

'In the second-half, it was always going to be that whoever scored first would win the game.'

Opposite.
Dundee United striker David Goodwillie opens the cup final scoring as County 'keeper Michael McGovern is caught off his line.
(*Press & Journal*)

Overleaf.
United's Craig Conway beats County goalkeeper Michael McGovern and the Cup is on its way to Tannadice.
(*Ken Macpherson*)

And so it proved. United's threats during several attacks finally bore fruit just after an hour had been played. Michael McGovern, the County goalkeeper, entered the vacant area that opened up before him as Morgaro Gomis, the clever United playmaker, launched a speculative ball forward.

The ball bounced awkwardly for McGovern, forcing him to step out of his area to head it clear; it fell to David Goodwillie, whose quick-thinking brought an early return towards goal and the goalkeeper turned to see it hit the back of his net.

McGovern, a Northern Ireland international, had already bagged two Scottish Cup winners' medals from his time with Celtic, although he was on the bench on both occasions. Winning a third for actually participating would, he admitted, have been sweeter.

It was an unfortunate moment for the County keeper, the kind that changes the course of a game, and he later explained that he had failed to make proper contact with the ball in his attempt to clear the danger.

'I came out to try and help,' he said, 'but I didn't get much purchase on the ball to head clear. Every goal you lose, you think later that you could have done better, but Goodwillie finished it off brilliantly.'

Worse was to follow, with the Tannadice side's 25,000-strong tangerine army experiencing a special ecstasy, and somehow finding a louder collective voice.

'Two further United goals, both scored by Craig Conway, were to follow – in the 75th and 86th minutes – by which time the Staggies had collapsed, their dream disintegrated and dead.

But there were no recriminations. Why should there be? They had had the more difficult route to the final and their achievement had been gargantuan.

'Dundee United deserved to win the game,' Adams conceded. 'They played well and created opportunities and we didn't do that on the day.'

There were tears from those in County colours on the pitch and in the Hampden stands as this dramatic season reached its conclusion. But there was applause from the supporters of both sides for the Staggies. Remember, they had entered league football as recently as 1994, the year United had recorded their previous, and only, Scottish Cup triumph.

POST-FINAL REFLECTIONS

Anyone wandering into the first-floor function suite of the Westerwood Hotel, Cumbernauld, at eight o'clock on the evening of 15 May 2010, could have been forgiven for thinking they were caught up in a wedding reception or a celebration of someone winning the Lottery.

The mood was bright and breezy as the Ross County players, their partners, the management team and the board and administrators of the club reflected on the day and their wonderful season.

Nothing and no-one would be allowed to dampen the spirits of these Highland heroes.

Certainly Martin Scott, known to all as Jimmy, would not permit it. His infectious sense of fun ensured it was laughs all the way as he launched a series of impromptu scenarios that at one point brought him to the centre of the room, right shoe placed against his ear like one of those original brick-sized mobile phones from the 1980s.

'Wir ye at the game?' he shouted into the shoe. 'Ye wir! Ye what? Ye left efter ten minutes?'

It may have been a reflection of how the team had under-performed that day, but it didn't matter. After all, how many players could boast that they appeared in a Scottish Cup final at Hampden during their careers?

'What's the point in being down?' he said in quiet reflection. 'The season's over, we reached a cup final with some incredible results. We are a First Division club and for us to reach the final of a national competition is something to be proud of.

'We're all disappointed and some of us will say, "I wish I could have done better," but we played an SPL club who finished third in their league and they were the better side on the day.'

Scott, as hard-working a midfielder as can be found anywhere in the First Division, had joined County four years earlier from Livingston, his home-town team, where he and Derek Adams first met. Paul Lambert, the former Celtic and Scotland midfielder, was manager but quit Livingston after only a few months in what was his first managerial job. The West Lothian side were relegated and Scott found his way north to join County.

'I wanted to re-build my career' he said, 'and Derek and George Adams constructed a really good squad of young talent.

'The gaffer played with us at Victoria Park, but as soon as he went into the manager's job we all gave him the respect he deserves. Some of us had been at Premier League clubs and he has encouraged us and given us belief that we can

still do well in football, despite the knocks we may have taken.'

Invariably, the post-mortem on the final drifted in and out of the conversation as frequently as another County player headed for the bar in the Westerwood Hotel. There was little point after such a glorious season, however, for self-criticism.

The most compelling argument for United's victory is that they were the better team, though not, according to Paul Di Giacomo, a late County substitute, because his team-mates had frozen in the heat of Hampden.

'The Celtic game was a bigger occasion,' he said. 'Celtic gave us time on the ball and we have good players. Credit Peter Houston, the United manager, and his staff. They obviously saw we have good players on the ball and didn't allow them to play. Our ball players did not have the time to control the game as they did against Celtic. I thought their two boys in the middle of the park were excellent and the wingers were a good outlet for them.'

Iain Vigurs, one of the midfielders who simply could not find their stride, was honest in his appraisal of the proceedings at the national stadium.

'Dundee United played very well, they got into our faces and didn't give us any time to play,' he said. 'We didn't play our usual game and we were all over the place in the first-half. I don't think the expectations of the fans had anything to do with it. We have played in front of big crowds before.'

Scott Morrison, a loser in a Scottish Cup final with Dunfermline, insisted: 'We went into this final believing we would win. Little Ross County believed we would win. That says it all.'

For Dave Siegel, the Ross County chairman, it was the culmination of a dramatic year at the helm at Victoria Park, having been introduced to the job towards the end of season 2008–09, when the Staggies were battling for First Division survival.

His telecommunications company, HIGHnet, sponsored the team's shirts, and when Roy MacGregor relinquished the chairmanship to devote more time to his own business, it was to Siegel he turned.

MacGregor was very persuasive, convincing his friend that the job would need around half a day of his time each week.

'We had to go down to Morton on the last day of the season,' Siegel remembered, 'and win to ensure that we stayed up. And that's what we did.'

Siegel noted when he took over that the club had drifted away from the fans and he set about rectifying what he considered a lapse. It had become the board on one side, the supporters on the other.

At home games, as well as his boardroom duties he took to walking around the ground meeting the fans and hearing their observations and complaints.

'We have now brought the supporters much closer to us,' he said. 'Without them, we don't have a football club. We're entertainers, they're the audience and we need them to turn up.'

It would not then be an understatement to suggest that, from being in such a precarious position as they were in season 2008–09, Siegel did not expect to be alongside MacGregor in heading the County delegation at Hampden in successive months a year later.

Dave Siegel, who stepped down as Ross County chairman days after the cup final to concentrate on his business and family commitments.
(*Press & Journal*)

Within a week of that great occasion, however, he had stepped down, citing a need to devote more time to his family and business commitments, and reminding his associates that he had agreed to chair the board for just one year.

'The camaraderie at the club was a big factor in carrying us through,' he insisted. 'The wages are pretty much the same in the squad and the players are treated well. They are boys who hadn't been able to establish themselves at other clubs and we have embraced them. I saw the change in some of the players in one season and they have developed into very good professionals.

'As a club, Ross County could survive in the Premier League, where there is a big gap between the top four or five clubs and the bottom four or five. I firmly believe there isn't much between them and the top four or five in the First Division. We can compete.

'As for the cup final, we went to Hampden not for our day in the sun but to win. I was bitterly disappointed, but immensely proud of our players for getting us there. What an experience.

'There was a rivalry between the fans that was friendly and without any of the bitterness sometimes witnessed on these occasions. It was fantastic.'

So, how did some of Scotland's leading football writers, there to report the action and the reaction for their newspapers, record the event?

Keith Jackson, of the *Daily Record*, wrote: 'Yes, the chance was presented to him [Goodwillie] on a silver platter by the unfortunate Mick McGovern, who chose the most inconvenient moment possible to be struck down by brain freeze as he stepped over the edge of his own box.

'But even though the keeper panicked before fluffing a header straight to the United young gun, McGovern should not be too hard on himself... If only that ball had arrived a split-second earlier, if only he could have clutched it in his grasp before stepping over that white line? Who knows how this remarkable, romantic Highland fling might have ended? But the truth is, just as so many of his team-mates were running on empty for their big day, McGovern's luck had dried up too. Of all of United's players it just HAD to be Goodwillie who was on hand and even then, the finish which this outrageously talented 21-year-old conjured up took the breath away.'

Press & Journal writer Michael Gannon opined: 'To the casual observer it must have seemed that the Staggies failed to turn up. In truth, they had already scaled their mountain.

'They did it with victories against SPL clubs en route to Hampden and by achieving one of the unlikeliest results in the competition's history when Celtic were put to the sword.

'Winning the trophy was to prove just one fanciful leap too far – but the Staggies went out with their heads held high.'

Bill Leckie, writing in the *Sun*, said: 'The fans turned up. The players didn't.'

That's the story of Ross County's Cup Final day in the sun, in seven stark words.

'But as Derek Adams and Craig Brewster went round each of their men

Cup final tears... Richard Brittain's expression reflects the immediate post-final emotions of County players and fans at the end of 90 minutes. (*Ken Macpherson*)

with hugs and handshakes, both reminded them of something they should never forget.

'That they'd earned the right to be there in the first place. And that in doing so, they'd given so many a trip they'll treasure forever.'

The *Scotsman*'s Stephen Halliday's critique made for painful reading for Staggies fans.

'United's tactical discipline not only ensured a lack of incident for long periods of the afternoon, it also left Derek Adams' First Division shock troops bereft of the bite and vibrancy which had seen them memorably lay waste to the Scottish Cup ambitions of Hibs and Celtic in previous rounds. By giving Ross County the respect they deserved, United succeeded in removing any threat they might have posed.'

In *Scotland on Sunday*, Tom English chronicled the cup final thus: 'This was a day to remind us that there is only so much romance to go around on cup final day, only one fairytale story that can be told.

'We lived through their hype and their hoopla all week long, their talk of Highland Clearances and their stories of pilgrims coming to Hampden from the four corners of the globe. Oh yes, County brought their fans and their colour and their noise, but their opponents brought the only currency that counts on these occasions: goals. Salute the passion of the underdogs, but salute Dundee United all the more.'

Alex Montgomery, of the *Daily Mail*, wrote: 'This was to have been the day fairytales came true – when little Ross County would pull off the most spectacular victory ever witnessed in a Scottish Cup final.

'But if the Highlanders' heart beat strongly, their only real armory was sheer effort and that was never going to be good enough to deny Dundee United their first major trophy for 16 years.'

Montgomery may have been accurate in his summation of those 90 energetic minutes of football, but whatever the result, the sheer pride of the family of Highlanders who made that historic trip to Glasgow was undiminished.

THE FANS' STORIES

Every Ross County supporter had his or her story of the big day. Whether they had travelled from Tain or Timbuktu, from Alness or Australia, the Highland army had answered the call and gathered at Hampden for the final push.

There were also those with extra special reasons for being there and, like 11-year-old Emma Cameron, made superhuman efforts to play their part.

It was in November 2009 that the diagnosis of a problem in her right leg revealed a tumour. Less than three months later, Emma's leg was amputated, but this battling young Staggie attended the Scottish Cup semi-final win over

A proud Emma Cameron walks out on to the Hampden pitch with Andy Barrowman in front of more than 45,000 excited cup final fans.

Celtic in her wheelchair, then had her spirits lifted when she was invited to be a club mascot on the big day.

Emma's father Alan, born and bred in Dingwall, moved to Torrance, East Dunbartonshire, in 1984 and was as determined that his daughter would experience the thrill of the cup final.

Motivated by the opportunity, Emma practiced her walking and made the 400 metre journey unaided from her home to her local church. Like her team, she was ready for Hampden.

But would she make it? In the week leading up to the cup final, Emma underwent regular chemotherapy, which ended just two days before the big game. Nothing was going to prevent her from keeping her appointment with the Staggies, and when she arrived at the stadium at 1.45pm with her dad and her sister Rachel, her heart was beating fast.

Changed into Ross County colours, Emma took her place alongside the other mascots chosen to walk out, each holding the hand of a player, and she was delighted to have been paired-up with Andy Barrowman, friendly and helpful and allowing Emma all the time she needed to make her way down the tunnel and out on to the lush grass of the Hampden pitch.

Up in the stands, her friends and family burst with pride to see her: no wheelchair, no crutches, no walking sticks. It was a moment to savour, one they and Emma would never forget.

Fraser Rankine, raised in Inverness and Alness but a resident of the Borders since 1991, was joined by supporters of Ayr United, Brechin City, Hibs and Rangers – all Borderers – on the road to the final.

Fraser, a healthy working lives adviser with NHS Borders, had spent the weeks leading up to the big day juggling hospital appointments as he awaited an operation to replace a cruciate ligament in his knee.

Officials at Victoria Park and at the SFA expressed surprise at his intentions to be there, each of them inquiring: 'will you be fit enough?'

'The club finally were in a position to help me out,' said Fraser, 'and the best compromise was to allocate me an aisle seat so I could keep my gammy leg straight out. On the morning of my operation, 5 May, I still hadn't completed the deal so phoned the club. No problems; tickets sorted, paid for and in the post – a huge weight off my mind. On the eve of the final, I heard that my operation would go ahead on the 19 May. I was relieved I was able to experience such a wonderful day… even with my sore leg, though the operation was a success.'

Craig Maclean, alias Taffy, from the Inverness Ross County supporters, soaked up the pre-match atmosphere in Glasgow the night before the game, then kicked-off match day along with hundreds of other County fans on the Renfrew Ferry, now a permanently-moored music venue on the Clyde.

It was there that Highland bands, Hunky Dory and Torridon, performed as the fans rocked the boat and generally psyched themselves up for what was to happen a few hours later.

'Over the day I met friends and ex-pats now living in Australia and Tenerife who had travelled over to see their local team play in the final,' said

Taffy. 'My in-laws, who'd never been to a football match, travelled on a bus to Hampden, while my sister-in-law, who hadn't been to a game for years since becoming a mother was also there.

'It was a fantastic day, as I was joined by my brother – he and I had attended each round – and with lots of friends I hadn't seen since school and growing up in the Highlands. We were all standing together at Hampden Park, to witness history being made and see the first Highland club to ever reach a Scottish Cup final.

'Looking at 20,000 County fans waving flags, scarves and banners was a sight to behold and something I'll remember till the day I die. I was supposed to be with my wife in Inverness at a friend's wedding, but couldn't miss our day of history and kept my promise to return home right after the game to join her and the happy couple for the evening reception.

'I felt the atmosphere wasn't quite as good as the semi final, but this was

Staggies from opposite ends of Scotland: Rear Left to right they are: John Palmer (Newstead near Melrose), Fraser Rankine (Newstead and formerly Alness), Graeme Currie (Galashiels), Colin Dickson (St Boswells), and Roger Spark (Lauder) Front from left to right: Kathy Sutherland (Alness), Jenny Rankine (St Boswells and formerly Alness), Heather Rankine (Newstead), Cameron Rankine (Newstead) and Michael Palmer (Newstead).

Craig Maclean in his County strip, ejoys the atmosphere of Hampden with his brother Alan, from Ullapool, and his in-laws, Mary and Howard Bell, from Alness.

to be expected with so many supporters who'd never been to a football match and not knowing our regular songs and chants.

'I was proud to have been there supporting my team. Yes, we were disappointed, but we'd won our cup final, so to speak, in the semi-final with Celtic where nobody – myself included – gave us a chance. Well done the Staggies!'

There is a foreign legion of fans who follow the fortunes of Ross County. The Scottish Cup semi-final and the final prompted a pilgrimage to Hampden by hundreds of supporters who had travelled tens of thousands of miles.

Predictably, many of those who had spent their savings flying to Scotland for the semi-final did not reckon on their vocal services being required a few weeks later, which meant they had to support from afar, courtesy of live television coverage of County versus Dundee United.

The Norwegian Ross County supporters fell into that category. Based on the island of Stord, on Norway's west coast between Bergen and Stavanger, some of them have made more than 20 visits to Victoria Park since they set up in 1993.

So why County as their team of choice? Many regulars at a local pub on Stord had a favourite English club, but there was a group thought it would be fun to support a small club from the lower divisions in Scotland.

Jan Hevroy, one of their number, explained: 'We hung the league tables on a board. One of us, Inge, put a scarf over his eyes and with a dart in his hand, he pointed it at a club called Ross County.

Little happened until 2001, when one of Roy MacGregor's employees from Global Energy Group, Gavin McDonald, in the area on business, spotted a Ross County scarf hanging in the pub.

'Our first match at Victoria Park was on 16 March 2002,' said Jan, who sponsors manager Derek Adams, 'after which we've had three or four trips

every year, twice, unfortunately, when the game was postponed. We have calcu-
lated that 86 Norwegians have visited Dingwall. Robert Delis has been over 22
times, while I am second in the table with 21 trips.

'When we leave Stord for Dingwall, we have to start early. We have a boat
trip with a fastboat for about an hour-and-a-half. That takes us to Flesland
Airport, Bergen, from where we fly to Aberdeen. The travelling time is about
nine hours.'

Determined to be part of the cup final occasion, the Vikings gathered at
the pub where they first thought of forming a supporters' club, to watch the
game on television.

'We turned the whole place into a Ross County pub for the day,' said Jan.

Simeon Ewing was another Staggie who watched the big game from a pub,
but he was in the Ukrainian capital of Kiev.

A Dingwall native, Simeon, who works for a Christian charity in
Rzhyshchiv, a two-hour drive from Kiev, was at the semi-final against Celtic
and on the way back north he stopped at a petrol station outside Perth and
bumped into Michael Gardyne.

Simeon had to return to the Ukraine on 28 April and was unable to be at
the final, which meant he was grateful to the Golden Gate pub in Kiev for
having the satellite television coverage on which he could watch his beloved
team against Dundee United.

Jan Hevroy (left) and fellow
members of the Norwegian
branch of the Ross County
supporters club gather
outside their local pub for
cup final viewing on TV.

Simeon Ewing, home from the Ukraine, and Fraser Polworth meet County hero Michael Gardyne (right) after the game against Celtic.

'My dad's birthday present was a ticket for the game,' he said, 'and he had a great day out. He particularly enjoyed the "last one out, turn off the lights" sign somewhere on the road out of the Highlands.

'An Australian friend and I missed the first 12 minutes of the final because we couldn't find the pub at first and then the two of us sat in a huge, empty room watching TV as a group of Londoners viewed the Chelsea-Portsmouth FA Cup final next door.

'It was a hard, lonely afternoon watching from so far away knowing the atmosphere in the middle of 20,000 Hampden Highlanders must have been something else altogether. It made the outcome harder to take, missing out on all the fun of the big day out. But we're all extremely proud of the boys for a magnificent run, and a lot of folks in Central Ukraine have got pretty interested in Ross County over the course of the season.'

Quite what Stephen Gair's fellow travellers on the flight from Bermuda to London on 13 May thought as they encountered this strange man decked out in a flag and wearing a red County away strip, is not known.

But the lone Staggie, a butcher in Bermuda, was soon in more familiar company when he strolled through London's Gatwick Airport at seven o'clock in the morning.

He said: 'I came across supporters from Dubai, then another from Singapore and, on the flight to Glasgow, I sat next to another Staggie from Singapore, though he was originally from Tain. It was almost as if we were just going doon the road to see a game.'

Stephen, from Conon Bridge, moved to Bermuda in 1989 and was happy to spend a weekend in Scotland to support his team, despite the result.

Stephen Gair, a lone
Staggie from Bermuda, flies
the Ross County colours
from the West Indies to
the West of Scotland.

'The crowd was great, the United fans were good and the atmosphere was tremendous,' he said.

Neil and John Ross may have been born and bred in England, where they still live, but they had special reason to make the pilgrimage to Hampden for the cup final; their late father Bill, from Alness, was a County player in the club's infancy.

Bill Ross led an interesting and full life after starting out as an apprentice gardener, working some of the time at Balnagown Castle, during which time he met the Queen Mother.

But the young man was also a sportsman and played for Alness and Ross County between 1933 and 1937, when he decided to leave the Highlands to join the police force at St Helens, Lancashire. He continued to play football and represented the police in several cup finals at grounds at Everton, Manchester City and Tranmere Rovers.

Bill's police career was interrupted in 1942 when he joined the Royal Marines and took part in many assignments throughout the Second World War, including action on Sword Beach on D-Day.

Neil explained that, while he and John, both now living in Ipswich and there because of their father's career, had witnessed Ross County's stunning semi-final win over Celtic, his son Craig had been unable to be there.

'John and I felt we needed to be at the semi-final in support of the team and to our father's memory,' he said. 'As soon as we made it through to the final, our diaries were cleared and the flight tickets booked for us, and Craig, to attend. Nothing was going to keep us away from this once-in-a-lifetime event.'

Bill Ross, a Hampden
tribute from his family.

Many years after Bill Ross left his native Highlands in search of a new challenge south of the border, he was once more to meet the Queen Mother, this time as Deputy Chief Constable of Suffolk when he went to Buckingham Palace to receive the Queen's Police Medal, an occasion which afforded them a little time to reminisce.

'John and I became Ipswich Town supporters,' Neil revealed, 'and season ticket holders in the belief that while you inherit one team, you can adopt another and we have always kept a special place in our affections for Ross County, given my father's connections with the club.'

Don Ross has never forgotten his Highland roots. The family came from Hilton of Cadboll, near Tain, and all of them – father Donald and his brothers, William, Hector and John Angus – played for their village team the Seaside Rovers. All were Ross County supporters, too.

Don and his family left for Australia in 1966 when he was just eight years old and he had been back to his native land only twice, until May 2010.

Don, a businessman in Melbourne, watched County beat Celtic in the semi-final on television and decided there and then that he had to be at the final. It would, he believed, be a once-in-a-lifetime experience that could not be missed.

With his best friend Les Smith, an Aussie who'd never been to a football

match, for company, Don was extra-keen for him to witness how passionate the Scots are about the game and for him to sample the company and hospitality of true Highlanders.

The Ross family setting off for the final: Craig, John and Neil.

With his tickets bought over the internet, and arrangements made for two County tops to be waiting for them at the Hilton Hotel, Glasgow, the intrepid pair set off.

'We flew from Melbourne to Sydney, then to Bangkok,' said Don, 'where there were some tensions at the airport because of the Red Shirt protesters.'

The Red Shirts, drawn from rural masses and the urban poor, had demonstrated against the Thai government for several weeks, calling for new elections, before being subdued by the military.

'We found out four people had been killed at that point and 46 injured during protests in the city and we were concerned we might be caught up in it all, but on we went to London and finally to Glasgow the night before the game.

'The taxi driver who picked us up at the airport, a fanatical Celtic supporter, told us County had deserved to beat them in the semi-final and he wished us all the best for the following day.

'We learned there was a gathering of about 650 supporters on the former Renfrew Ferry before the game and headed down there. We went to the game on one of the special buses hired by the club and were amazed to find how

From Melbourne to Mount Vernon: Don Ross (left) and Les Smith.

friendly the two sets of supporters were towards each other, with many Dundee United supporters wishing us good luck. It was a fabulous day.'

But if the 20,000 supporters of Ross County were proud of how their team had eclipsed all expectations and reached the final of Scottish football's most prestigious cup competition, so too were all directly associated with the club, none more so than Roy MacGregor, who embraced the occasion with all the verve and vigour he is known to possess.

He summed up 15 May 2010 thus: 'It was a privilege to be out on the Hampden pitch before the start, to see our supporters and to hear the level and genuine warmth of their voices as they sang and cheered.

'It wasn't our turn this time and you have to accept you weren't the best team on the day. We can't now look back.

'Like sipping a good whisky, we've had a taste of something very special by competing in the final of such a prestigious tournament, one of the oldest in the world, and we want more.

'We have to forget the years since we entered the Scottish Football League, accept that expectations have risen and that there is a whole new generation of supporters looking forward. The responsibility is on the board of directors to deal with that. We're all in it together: board, management, players and community.

'Eighty-one teams set out in the Scottish Cup competition. We finished second.'

Opposite.
Roy MacGregor greets 20,000 fellow County fans at Hampden before the cup final kick-off. (*Ken Macpherson*)

THE ROSS COUNTY SQUAD
2009–10

Goalkeepers

Michael McGovern started out at Celtic and had a spell with Dundee United before being snapped up by Ross County. Born on 12 July 1988, the 6ft 2in Irishman has established himself as the No. 1 at Victoria Park.

Joe Malin, born on 13 July 1988, came through the youth ranks at Celtic alongside David Marshall, whose career took him from Parkhead to Norwich City and Cardiff City, as well as international honours for Scotland. Joe moved to Ross County under-19s in 2005 and he has progressed through the ranks to the senior squad.

Defenders

Grant Smith is one of the First Division's most experienced players, having played with a long list of clubs, including Reading, Hearts and Dundee United, and in Finland and Australia. A versatile player with a physical presence, Grant was born on 5 May 1980.

Scott Boyd clinched a permanent move to County after a loan period from Partick Thistle at the beginning of the 2007–08 season. He signed in January 2008 and has matured into a player whose name will be among the first on the manager's team sheet. Born on 4 June 1986, Scott is highly regarded in First Division football.

Graham Girvan, born on 24 June 1990, came up through the County youth ranks and, having captained the under-19 team in 2008–09, was handed his first professional contract. He has already featured in the first team.

Alex Keddie embarked on his professional football career while part of the Leeds United squad that clinched the FA Youth Cup. He later studied at Glasgow Caledonian University, where he gained an honours degree in chartered surveying. Born on 23 January 1981, he also played with Stranraer and is a powerful presence at the heart of the County defence.

Gary Miller, born on 15 April 1987, and formerly of Livingston, joined County after impressing during an earlier loan spell at Victoria Park. In that period, he played a vital role in County's Second Division championship-winning season.

Scott Morrison has seen professional service at Aberdeen and Dunfermline Athletic. Born on 23 May 1984, Scott was capped a dozen times for Scotland at under-21 level and turned out for the Pars in the 2006–07 Scottish Cup final. Able to operate at left-back or on the left of midfield, his experience has proved invaluable to County.

Steven Watt has sampled life as a professional footballer at Chelsea, where he made his debut against Scunthorpe United in the FA Cup. He moved to Swansea City, but before and after he had loan spells with Barnsley and Inverness Caledonian Thistle. Born on 1 May 1985, Steven's experience has been relied upon in the centre of the Victoria Park defence.

Midfielders

Born on 24 September 1983, Richard Brittain has been a key component in the County midfield since moving from St Mirren. He was captain of the Livingston side that included County boss Derek Adams, and his experience at the top level of Scottish football has given County an extremely useful player to have in their ranks.

Ross Grant, a Tain lad born on 22 September 1990, is another player who has come through the Ross County youth system, making the jump from under-19s to first team in 2009–10, and is reckoned to be one for the future by the management team at Victoria Park.

Stuart Kettlewell was one of six new signings for County ahead of the 2009-10 season and is a powerhouse of the midfield, energetic and tough-tackling. Born on 4 June 1984, Stuart was captain at his previous clubs, Queen's Park and Clyde.

Paul Lawson, like others in the County squad, is a product of Celtic's youth system, after which he had spells at St Johnstone and St Mirren before his move to Dingwall. Born on 15 May 1984, Paul is a cultured midfielder whose passes frequently un-pick opposition defences.

Daniel Moore is a local lad from the Black Isle who first caught the eye playing for the under-13 side when he famously scored a goal from the halfway line against Inverness Caledonian Thistle's youngsters. He had a spell on loan at Peterhead, helping them win a place in the Second Division play-offs in 2008–09.

Martin Scott's goal in the Scottish Cup semi-final against Celtic was just reward for the dedicated and enthusiastic midfielder, known as Jimmy. Born on 15 February 1986, and previously at Livingston, his energy and work-rate is important to the County side

Iain Vigurs, an Aberdonian born on 7 May 1988, had first-team experience at Inverness Caledonian Thistle and, before that, at Elgin City with whom he made his debut at just 15-years-old. Iain can operate anywhere along the midfield and is regarded as an exceptional talent.

Forwards

Andy Barrowman's career started at Birmingham City, after which he saw action at Kilmarnock, Queen of the South, Ross County and Inverness Caledonian Thistle. Now in his second spell at Victoria Park, Andy, born on 27 November 1984, helped the Staggies win the Second Division title in 2007–08 by hitting 29 goals.

Steven Craig's stunning strike against Celtic in the Scottish Cup semi-final underlined his scoring prowess and the experience gained at Falkirk, Motherwell, Aberdeen and Livingston, not to say a loan period at Dundee. Born on 5 February 1981, Steven's worth to the County side should not be understated, as that semi-final goal highlighted.

Paul Di Giacomo, born on 30 June 1982, was a long-time regular in the Kilmarnock team before being transferred to Airdrie United. He joined County in the summer of 2009 and is highly rated as a penalty box player with an eye for goal.

Garry Wood, another Aberdonian in the squad, was born on 27 January 1988, and arrived at Victoria Park in the summer of 2009 having been released by Inverness Caledonian Thistle. His physique has proved more than useful to County up front, where opposition defenders can't take their eyes off him.

Michael Gardyne knew what he was taking on when he joined the Staggies, as he'd already spent a loan period from Celtic with the club in 2005–06. Born on 23 January 1986, he was with Morton before moving back north, where his vigour and vim allied to his skill and courage – all attributes which brought him Scotland caps at under-17 and under-19 levels – have made him a huge favourite with the fans.